150 SELF-PUBLISHING QUESTIONS ANSWERED

ALLI'S WRITING, PUBLISHING, AND BOOK MARKETING TIPS FOR INDIE AUTHORS AND POETS

ALLIANCE OF INDEPENDENT AUTHORS

with

M.L. RONN

Series Editor

ORNA A. ROSS

FOREWORD

BY ORNA ROSS

Thanks to self-publishing, there has truly never been a better time to be an author. Publishing a book has never been easier. Social media and other tech innovations make it possible to reach readers all over the world. Authors are strengthening each other through co-operation and collaboration.

At the same time, it is also true that writing and publishing are as hard as ever. Writing a good book is a high-order challenge. So is publishing well, especially finding and connecting with the right readers. You can quickly find yourself lost in the land of confusion, especially at the beginning, as you negotiate some steep learning curves. That's where this book and ALLi, the Alliance of Independent Authors, come in.

If you haven't yet heard of ALLi (pronounced ally, "al-eye"), it's a global, nonprofit association for self-publishing authors. Our mission is ethics and excellence in self-publishing and we bring together thousands of indie authors all over the world who are united behind this mission. All our profits are reinvested back into the organization for the benefit of our members and the wider indie author community.

Our intention is to empower today's authors with the knowledge and mindset shift needed to become the creative directors of their books, and of profitable author businesses. For our members this means private forums, discounts and deals, a member-care and watchdog desk, and other benefits. And ALLi also provides an outreach service to the wider author community, curating, monitoring, and campaigning in seven key territories across the world.

As you can imagine, all of this means answering a lot of questions. Back in 2014, ALLi launched its #**AskALLi** campaign, in which we pledge to answer, with evidence-based authority, *any* self-publishing *any* author might have. One popular highlight of that campaign is the monthly **Member Q&A** in which Michael (ML Ronn) and I answer our members' most pressing questions.

Michael has done us all a wonderful service in authoring this book, which curates those questions and answers into one convenient collection. Organized across the seven stages of publishing—editorial, design, production, distribution, marketing, promotion, and rights licensing—together with sections on writing and running an indie author business, it addresses more than 150 of the most common and complex queries.

Whether you're a beginning writer wondering how to publish, an indie author who's published a book and is ready for the next level, or an established author who's making a living—or even a killing!—from your writing, you'll find a lot of value here. Michael's clear, trusted, and accessible answers will guide your way, ease your journey, flatten your learning curves, introduce you to strategies and tools you may have overlooked, and save you time and money.

In the words of Michael's own popular YouTube channel and website, AuthorLevelUp.com, this book will enable you to level up across all the stages of the writing and publishing process. Keep it close by as you work and dip into it, as needed.

If you have further questions arising from what you read here, or a question that isn't answered in this book, ALLi would love to hear from you. Members: drop by our private Facebook forum, or send a private query to the Member Care Desk. Non-members, drop us a query anytime at SelfPublishingAdvice.org/Contact.

Until we hear from you, happy writing and publishing and may all your questions be answered.

Orna Ross

Director, Alliance of Independent Authors

London 2020

WHAT YOU WILL LEARN IN THIS BOOK

INTRODUCTION BY M.L. RONN

Every writer's journey begins with a question. Many questions, actually.

What's my first step? How do I publish a book? How do I write it? How do I sell it?

As an aspiring writer, I had many questions. The more answers I found, the more questions I had!

I learned the hard way that not every answer you find is a good one. In fact, I found a lot of bad advice. Sometimes, I didn't know if advice was good *or* bad.

Enter the Alliance of Independent Authors (ALLi for short, pronounced "al-eye").

I discovered ALLi in 2012 while searching for resources on how to self-publish my first book. I was intrigued by ALLi's description as a global nonprofit association for authors with a mission of ethics and excellence in self-publishing. I also loved how ALLi shone a light on shady companies who tried to take advantage of fledgling writers like me.

I was also intrigued by the sheer amount of helpful information they provided to writers for free: blogs, books, podcasts, conferences, a Facebook group, and so much more.

After reading a few blog articles, I became a member. After meeting ALLi's Director, Orna Ross, I found her enthusiasm and passion for helping writers infectious. All these years later, I am still a member of ALLi because I believe in the organization's mission.

I also appreciate and admire the ALLi member community—ambitious self-published writers trying to help one another. I've been a part of many writing communities, but there isn't one quite like ALLi.

Through being a member and experiencing the benefits for myself to further my own author business, I became a believer in ALLi's ability to assist any writer to become the creative director of their books and their business.

I have made it a focus to help as many people learn about ALLi as possible because I believe ALLi can help them, just like it helped me when I was an aspiring writer with no clue how to write or publish a book.

A little about ALLi, a little about me

In the publishing community, I'm known as Michael La Ronn. As I write this, I am ALLi's Outreach Manager. Since ALLi's HQ is in the United Kingdom, with members all over the world, like its other ambassadors I spread the good word about ALLi to all my friends in my country and state, and I encourage businesses that have services for writers to consider joining ALLi's roster of approved services.

Since 2018, I have co-hosted the #AskALLi Member Q&A Facebook Live show and podcast with Orna, where we answer our members' most burning publishing questions every month. Since its inception in 2012, this question-and-answer session has solved more than a thousand member problems in publishing, writing, marketing, and more.

The podcast is part of the #**AskALLi** campaign, which pledges to answer *any* question *any* self-publishing author might have, using its extensive network of blog posts, podcast episodes, videos, and books. This program is addressed to paying ALLi members, who can submit their question through a form in the member zone of the ALLi website.

However, we publish the audio and video of the show online for free so that any self-publisher may listen and view, learning from our members' experiences.

There are few questions that ALLi hasn't seen and heard. For any questions that Orna and I can't answer, we have world-class advisors to draw from who have immense influence and expertise in publishing.

As for me and why I am qualified to write this book—I have written over fifty books of science fiction & fantasy and nonfiction for writers. I also host a popular weekly YouTube channel for writers called "Author Level Up," that, at time of writing, has over 25,000 subscribers, nearly one million views, and over two million minutes watched per year. Every minute of every day, someone is watching one of my writing videos on YouTube.

I built my writing business while working a full-time job in insurance, raising a family, and attending law school classes in the evenings. I also have a weekly podcast called "The Writer's Journey" that chronicles my experiences as a working writer, and a daily podcast called "Writing Tip of the Day" that provides a crisp writing tip in just two to three minutes.

I share my experiences and advice I've learned because I want to help writers succeed.

But enough about me. Let's talk about you and what you're going to learn in this book.

How to use this book

This book gathers 150+ of the most common self-publishing questions across the seven stages of publishing. You can read it from start to finish, or skip around to questions that interest you.

- The **Writing Books** section covers all things writing, writing craft, and publishing productivity.
- The **Editorial** section covers self-editing and working with different kinds of editors.
- The **Book Design and Formatting** section addresses book cover design, common questions about working with a cover designer, and the nuts and bolts of e-book formatting and print book typesetting.
- The **Book Production and Distribution** section covers the questions that most frequently come up when uploading your book to self-publishing platforms and distributing to readers, such as ISBNs and retailer-specific issues.
- The **Book Marketing and Promotion** section covers questions about selling your book and getting it in front of readers.
- The **Book Rights and Licensing** section covers the importance of understanding your rights as an author and publisher, common copyright questions, and other scenarios you might encounter where you have an opportunity to license your work to another party.
- And finally, the **Resources** section gathers many free ALLi resources to help you delve deeper into any questions you might still have after reading.

Does this book answer every single self-publishing question in the universe? No, but I tried to get in as many as I could. I also limited the question set to "evergreen" questions—meaning the answers in this book will be as true ten years from now as they are today.

I wrote this book primarily to help our ALLi members, but I also wrote it to help writers in general with common questions they have. My hope is that it will continue to serve as a helpful resource for years to come.

(Fun fact: ALLi members receive this book for free. If you're not a member, join us today!)

You don't have to go the writing route alone. Help is just a page-turn away.

PART I

WRITING BOOKS

THE CRAFT OF WRITING BOOKS

How can I improve my writing craft?

Ah, the elusive, enigmatic, mind-maddening challenge of improving your writing.

Writing craft isn't easy. Of all the necessary skills you need to master as an indie author, becoming a good writer has the biggest learning curve. It's not uncommon for it to take a writer *years* to learn how to write well.

My first tip on learning writing craft is to read often and across different genres. Even if you only write in one genre, reading widely allows you to take ideas and cross-pollinate them into your genre, which makes your voice and writing style fresh and original.

My second tip is to develop a loose system for studying the craft. You don't have to sit down and do a critical analysis of everything you read (actually, please don't do that), but taking some time to pay attention to passages you like and why you like them is a smart tip to improve your craft that costs you nothing.

Orna goes as far as recommending writers to read books they admire twice--once as a reader, for enjoyment. Then begin again and read as a writer, for learning. How did the author do what they did? What worked and what didn't, what was outstanding and what flopped, and, most importantly, why?

I'd be remiss if I didn't mention blogs, writing books, podcasts, YouTube channels, and courses—but there is no replacement for close reading and experiencing masterful craft firsthand.

No writing book in the world will truly teach you how to write at a Stephen King, Nora Roberts, or Margaret Atwood level.

Do I need an MFA/MA to write a book?

The short answer is no. The long answer is absolutely not. The slightly longer answer is it might even get in your way. It all depends on what kind of writer you are, and what drives you to write.

Master of Fine Arts (MFA) and Masters (of Arts) (MA) programs are graduate-level degrees whose focus is teaching writers how to write, but they primarily exist as a vehicle so that one can learn to teach the craft of writing to other writers. The major benefits of these programs are that they provide writers ample time and space to write, access to a supportive author network, and writing workshops to hone their craft.

While these programs have their merits, you don't need an MFA to write a book, just like you don't need a film degree to make movies, or a music degree to make music.

In today's publishing environment, everything an indie writer needs to be successful can easily be found on the internet.

For an investment of $1,000 on all of the best and current writing resources, you would potentially get a better, more practical education than you'd get from an MFA program—for a sliver of the cost. You won't get the campus experience, but I'd rather pay $1,000 and take my chances versus incurring tens of thousands in student debt that the campus experience provides. That's my personal opinion, of course.

· · ·

Should I write fiction or nonfiction?

Most new authors instinctively know what genres they want to write, but some don't. If you're one of those authors in the latter camp, it could be because you have wide-ranging interests, or because you're still trying to figure out what kind of author you want to be.

If you're in doubt about what you truly want to write, I recommend reading a truckload of books. Go to your local library, wander the stacks until you get dizzy, and read dozens and dozens of books. Find out which ones resonate with you most.

When you find that book that makes you feel fuzzy inside, like you could read it over and over again—write that.

You may think: "If I already read a book like this, why write it?"

Because no one will write a book like you can, that's why. Even if you write something similar, you're going to put your own unique spin on it, and readers appreciate that.

Invest in finding your true writing passion, and it will be worth your time.

How do I come up with story ideas?

Keeping your creative well full is an important way to maintain your vitality as a writer and avoid burnout.

The best way I've learned to never run out of ideas is to capture new ideas daily.

I use the Evernote app on my phone to write down ideas as they come to me. You can substitute Evernote with any common note-taking app. They all work the same.

I also value people-watching. Whenever I am in public, I pick one person out of a crowd and I ask: what's this person's story? I try to capture it in a few sentences.

I refer back to my Evernote app whenever I need inspiration. I find that old ideas blend together with new ones and create interesting hybrids.

Orna has long promoted the practice of F-R-E-E-writing (where the word free is an acronym for "fast, raw and exact-but-easy"), which is a proven method for idea generation that has a host of other benefits.

You can find out more about Orna's method of F-R-E-E-writing on her website.

However you decide to capture ideas—by hand, by app, or even by voice—remaining open to nature and your surroundings will help you develop a writer's eye.

Should I write to market or write my passion?

There is not a single indie author who doesn't have to wrestle with this question at least once. This is a deeply personal question that doesn't have a one-size-fits-all answer.

The goal is to find the intersection of art and commerce, something that you truly enjoy that also makes money. Maybe it means writing books in a few genres to see what you like and then doubling down on the ones you like the most that *also* have the best sales.

However, keep burnout top of mind as you negotiate this balance. I've talked to authors who strictly wrote to market and wish they hadn't because they burned out writing in genres they weren't passionate about. I've also talked to authors who don't make much money from writing because they're strictly writing their passions and not thinking enough about readers' needs.

Find the happy medium. It isn't as hard as you think. You've just got to be willing to explore and grow.

How do you research a book?

Research is fun. There's nothing better than learning about the story you want to write—except (maybe) writing it. I know some writers who prefer the research to the writing!

Some authors generally spend too much time on the research process. That said, research can be a time suck for any author and it can be hard to know where to stop.

Before you start, I recommend setting a time limit on your research. Maybe it's a couple of days, a week, or a month—whatever that looks like for you—but when the time limit is up, make a promise to yourself to start writing. You don't need months and months to research—only enough information to enable you to start writing. Then you research other details as they come up.

Depending on your genre, start with an Internet search on what you want to learn and go deeper from there.

There are two major story elements you will likely need to research: the world and the characters.

Let's say you want to research a historical fantasy novel that takes place in London during World War I. Here's what you might need to do:

- Read books on what it was like in London in the World War I years. You may be able to buy them online or at a local bookstore, check them out from your local library, or listen to audiobooks.
- Watch documentaries, television shows, movies, or YouTube videos about World War I London.
- See if your library has microfilms that may be related to your book's era. Microfilms are a goldmine.
- Find era-inspired images on Pinterest to get clarity on what the city looked like and what people wore.
- Listen to history podcasts that cover the World War I London era.
- Talk to people you know who live in London, or who have

relatives who lived there during World War I. Sometimes family stories can be a great inspiration for your novel.
- Post on social media that you want to interview someone with that background. You'll be surprised at who might see it.

Those are basic examples. Research greatly depends on your book and how much you already know. The less you know about the world you're writing in, the more research you will have to do.

Once you have finished your research, you'll need to gather all of your findings into a structure, which leads us to the next question…

What's the best way to organize my research?

Some writers like physical notebooks or scrapbooks to keep track of their research.

Some writers like to use a digital note-taking app like Evernote or Microsoft OneNote. These apps have "web clippers" that let you download content from the internet straight into your digital notebook.

And other writers like to use a writing app like Scrivener to track their research. Scrivener in particular has a nice corkboard and an index feature that helps you visualize your findings, and you can also move documents around to your heart's content.

However you decide to organize your research, there's no right or wrong way to do it. Just beware of the time it takes. If you find yourself spending several hours or days trying to get your research to look "pretty," it's probably time to start writing. Remember, when you are done writing, you'll likely no longer need your research, so treat it as a helpful tool, not a time-intensive process.

How do I outline my book?

There are as many novel-writing techniques as there are writers.

My approach has always been to expose myself to as many writing techniques as possible, and pick and choose what works for me.

I have included some useful links in the Resources section to get you some exposure to different outlining methods.

Full disclosure: outlining is not required for fiction, memoir, and other literary nonfiction. There are many writers who prefer to make up their stories as they go (I'm one of those writers), and that's perfectly valid. These are known as "pantsers," as opposed to "plotters," and there are resources to help you become a better pantser too.

Even if you don't outline in the beginning, you'll probably find yourself doing so at some point in the editing process.

For practical nonfiction, like how-to books, outlining is essential in order to communicate the value of your book to prospective readers. The best way to outline practical nonfiction is to look at all of your topics and structure them in a logical order that would make sense to a reader.

If you have a book on nutrition, for example, and you are smart about how you label your chapters, a prospective reader will see exactly what they will learn. They might see a chapter on vegetables, a chapter on fruits, a chapter on smoothies, another chapter on diets like Paleo or Keto, and so on.

This provides tremendous value to your readers and is a courtesy to them.

You can also supplement your research by looking at what other popular books are doing. A tip that has worked well for me is to title your chapters based on SEO research (SEO stands for search engine optimization). Let's say that you're passionate about smoothies and are going to spend some time writing about them in your book. Let's say that people are searching Google and Amazon for terms like "best smoothies for energy boosts." I'd title one of my chapters something like "Endless Energy: Best Organic Smoothie Recipes to Boost Your Energy."

You get the picture. Hook the reader with what they want and then you can deliver what you think they need.

What is NaNoWriMo and should I try it?

You may have heard a little term called NaNoWriMo (or one of its many spin-offs, like NaPoWriMo) and wondered what it meant...

It stands for National Novel Writing Month (and that spin-off is National Poetry Writing Month). NaNoWriMo is both the event and the namesake of the nonprofit organization that coordinates the event each year.

It began in the United States, but that "national" should now read "international," as it quickly spread around the world. Every November, novelists all over the globe sit down and try to write an entire 50,000-word novel in thirty days.

If that sounds challenging, that's because it is! But it's not an insurmountable challenge. Many aspiring writers became published writers with books they first wrote for a WRiMo.

While NaNoWriMo is marketed at novelists, there's nothing that says you can't write nonfiction or something else. All the WriMos are about the spirit and community of writers coming together to support and encourage one another—the "rules" are very relaxed.

If you're interested in participating, check the Resources section at the end of the book for links.

Should I include people of races/cultures other than my own in my stories?

This is a touchy subject that doesn't have a clear answer. No matter what answer I give, I risk angering 50 percent of the people reading this, but... I'm going to answer it anyway. (Controversy!)

Let's illustrate the problem with an example.

I am African-American. I've always wanted to visit Australia, but I've never been there. What if I want to write a novel that takes place in Australia from the perspective of an Aboriginal character?

The 100 percent honest answer is that I can do whatever I want, write whatever I want, and no one can stop me. It's a free world, and the country I live in (the United States of America) grants me freedom of speech, as do many countries around the world.

I'd better be careful, though.

For starters, I'd have to do a *lot* of research to be able to write a book about Australia, and even then it's likely I'd still get some details wrong about what it's like to live there. The smallest details that you don't even think about are the ones that readers will spot instantly.

More concerning, though, is the fact that I could unintentionally write something in the novel about my hero that would be offensive to Aboriginal people, *even though I wrote the novel in good faith.*

Let me repeat that last paragraph again, because it's the thing that many writers don't think about.

More concerning, though, is the fact that I could unintentionally write something in the novel about my hero that would be offensive to Aboriginal people, even though I wrote the novel in good faith.

I don't know what it's like to be an Aboriginal person, and quite frankly I doubt that Aboriginal people would appreciate an outsider trying to interpret them on the page unless that person did a fantastic job. Even then, a good-faith attempt could still be taken badly—they might *perceive* my writing as a misappropriation of their culture, even though I never intended for it to be taken that way.

Our entertainment industry is full of books, movies, and television shows that misstepped in their effort to portray minorities.

But all that said... there's nothing *stopping* me from doing this. Cancel culture and the risk of offending people aside, I can do whatever I want as a writer.

There are many writers who want to increase the visibility of minorities in fiction, and, in my opinion, that's a noble cause. But those same writers don't always do their research, and therefore they cause the opposite effect of their original intention.

The other side of the argument is that perhaps we live in a society that places too much weight on being politically correct. The counterargument is that for every writer that stumbles in portraying a minority on the page, there is another who succeeds. James Patterson is white, yet his Alex Cross series, the chronicles of an African-American detective, is one of the bestselling series of all time, and the books are incredibly authentic.

However you proceed, it's a personal issue for you to decide. Remember that your goal is to tell a good story. Don't let technicalities get in your way.

However, if you still choose to write a book about a culture or race other than your own, here are some best practices:

- Talk to people from that culture who are willing to help you. You would be surprised how many people *will* help you if you ask. Learn what is important to them, what is offensive to them, and what their experience with racism or discrimination has been like.
- Better yet, ask them to read your book and point out any details that don't make sense with their worldview. No one within any race is the same, but they can help you understand nuances that you will never find anywhere else.
- Supplement with research.
- Be prepared to anger people. No matter what you do and how diligent you are, someone is inevitably going to email you and

tell you that you don't have the right to write about X culture. Worse, that person may not ever read your book and may make baseless claims against you. Sometimes, the loudest detractors won't even be a part of the race they're accusing you of misappropriating.

In other words, if you're going to do this, do your very best and be ready for haters, even if you do everything right. The other side of this advice is that you better be prepared to own your mistakes and have some intense conversations.

If you make a misstep, treat it as a learning experience. After all, making mistakes and being open to our unconscious biases is how we progress as a society, especially as it pertains to race, gender, religion, sexuality, and minorities.

This path is not for everyone, but if you pursue it, good luck.

Should I write series or standalone novels?

This is primarily a fiction question, but it also applies to nonfiction.

In the realm of fiction, it's a universally accepted truth that series sell better. More books in the same universe equals more sales and more engaged readers. My series sell much, much better than my standalones.

The bigger question is what kind of series do you want to write? A continuous series where the reader has to read the books in chronological order, or a "standalone" series where readers can pick up anywhere? Or maybe your series takes place in the same world but with different characters. There's no wrong answer.

There's nothing bad about standalones, though. It's just harder to build a readership with them because readers have to start all over again with new characters and a different world. And if your standalones are in different genres or styles, it's even harder.

This is one of the reasons why literary novelists sell fewer copies, like for like, than writers in other genres. They are much more inclined to do standalones and to write in different styles.

For nonfiction, series are not required but always a smart choice. Even if your books are drastically different, tying them together with branding that makes sense can help readers see the value proposition and deliver what we publishers call "readthrough"—which means getting readers to read multiple (if not all) books in a series.

For example, this book you are reading is in *ALLi's Publishing Guides for Authors* series, which contains many comprehensive, 200+ page books about the most important aspects of self-publishing. All these guidebooks have similar covers. If you look at the entire series, the books cover every stage of the publishing process. If you like one, you'll probably like the others. Branding helps readers see that.

ALLi also does a series of *Ultimate Guides,* which are shorter books about particular aspects of publishing, like getting reviews or getting your books into libraries. The cover branding on this series is different so that readers can see at a glance which kind of book it is.

How many drafts should I do?

Welcome to the most frustrating answer in this book: you should do as many drafts as you need to do—but not too many.

Every writer is different, and I'm not going to give you a magic number. When it comes to your writing process, the only thing you should do is find the process that works best for you. I'll say this: yes, editing is an important part of the writing process, but sometimes writers take it too far.

Does your novel need 100 drafts? Absolutely not.

Will one draft do? Absolutely not if you're a beginner.

From my personal experience, the "one-draft novel" is indeed possible if you improve your skills and follow methods like Dean Wesley Smith's *Writing into the Dark*, but that takes time and learning.

Orna's opinion is that writing long-form books is hard, and some writers can only progress by giving themselves permission to write garbage in the first draft, knowing they'll sort it out later. It does help if you learn how to write a fair draft the first time, so that you don't have to do as many drafts. That may be paralyzing for a beginning writer.

In her words,

"That was me. I learned to write like this, using what Annie Lamott calls the 'shitty first draft' method. As a result, it took me a very long time, and many drafts, to deliver a book, and I have definitely been guilty of over-revising, doing fixes that feel important to me but have little effect on the reader's enjoyment or learning. As I write more, I'm learning to change that. Now I try to do a fair draft first time out and limit myself to two more passes, then I get it to the editor."

— ORNA ROSS, ALLI'S DIRECTOR

Orna is not alone. Too many writers get stuck in the black hole of revision, in my opinion. It's a good idea to not dwell there longer than you should. But exactly how many drafts you should do is an answer you'll have to work out for yourself.

How long should my book be?

Another irritating answer: as long as it needs to be... and no longer!

Don't let anyone tell you that a novel *has* to be 50,000 words or more. Many of these rules arose out of traditional publishing practices, where

70,000 words was the most profitable price point for publishers and booksellers. Such rules have no place in the age of digital publishing.

Look at some of the bestselling books in recent history (especially those taught in schools) and you'll see that many of them were novella length.

Write the book you feel compelled to write. If it's 50,000 words, great! If it's 100,000 words, that's fine too. If it's more than that, you might want to ask yourself whether you'd be better off breaking it down into two or more books.

While there's no perfect length for a book, there's no doubt that there is a trend these days for shorter books. Readers prefer them.

Another writer wants me to co-write a book with them. Should I?

Co-writing has become popular among self-published writers. Some co-writers make serious money. It can be lucrative—creatively and commercially—to combine the power of two writers' minds.

Why would you want to co-write a book in the first place?

Co-writing allows both authors to cross-pollinate their readers, pool their resources, and, in some respects, write a stellar book that neither of them could have written by themselves. Both writers expand their audiences and it's a win-win.

However, the key is making sure you have the *right* co-writer. After all, *you're going to be sharing royalties with this person for the rest of your lives.*

Why?

Because you'll co-own the copyright, and in most countries, copyright lasts for the author's life plus seventy years.

If you have a dispute with your co-writer, that's a long time to be angry at someone. Finding the right person is the first step, so choose wisely.

Once you find the right person, a contract is a must. Who is responsible for publishing the book? Who will distribute the royalties? What happens if you get into a fight over the cover, and who gets the final say? What happens if one of you dies? What happens if one of you dies before the book is finished? These are all questions a contract can help you answer.

Hopefully, you'll never need the contract, but if you do, it'll ensure you and your co-writer will be on the same page.

Can I write a book based on a real person?

Sometimes you might come across an irresistible story idea about a real person. Can you include that person in your story?

Generally speaking, no, but you *can* write about real people if you fictionalize them and change names and dates, assuming that it's not completely obvious who you're writing about.

The real issue is defamation. If you write something that someone perceives as false or injurious to their reputation, they can sue you, *especially* if you use their real name or create a character that is eerily similar.

What constitutes defamation? Only a court can answer that.

Some genres such as true crime, biography, and memoirs are especially dangerous for writers because the risk of defamation is high. It's nearly impossible to write books in those genres without covering real people.

Sometimes the risk of a defamation claim can come from family members too, so beware of airing your family's grievances... unless the people you are writing about are dead. You can't defame the dead (in most cases).

Anyway, taking real life and translating it onto the page is one of the most exciting parts of fiction. I don't mean to scare you.

Be inspired and have fun with your writing, but understand the potential risks when using real people.

. . .

Should I use a pen name?

Pen names have been popular since the beginning of time. Whether you should use one is a deeply personal choice, but consider my story.

M.L. Ronn is not my real name. It's another name for my writer persona, Michael La Ronn.

Michael La Ronn is not my real name either. I choose not to publish books under my real name because I have a professional career in insurance, and I don't want prospective clients seeing my fiction when they search for me on the internet. A pen name gives me a small layer of anonymity.

Some people may choose a pen name for other reasons, like being a female in a traditionally male-dominated genre, or for political reasons, like the fear of persecution in their country, or for privacy and freedom to write without having their real name associated with a genre like erotica.

The next question is whether you can keep a pen name truly private. The answer is probably not. No pen name is 100 percent secret. That's just the way things are. But if you desire privacy, you can do a pretty good job of concealing your identity if you really want to.

The next question is whether you should have multiple pen names. Some writers write all of their books under one pen name, even if those books are in multiple genres. Other writers create a pen name for each distinct genre that they write in.

Naturally, though, maintaining multiple pen names is more work, but some authors believe it's worth it so that the online retailer algorithms don't confuse readers by suggesting books to the wrong audience. You wouldn't want an algorithm to promote your thriller books to a romance audience, for example.

There are many factors to consider. If your business model is based on direct sales on your website, or your branding focuses on you the author versus your books, you'll approach it differently than someone who writes books in a single series with the same main character (à la Jack Reacher).

There's no right or wrong answer.

Should I release Book One right away or hold on to it until I have more books in a series?

This is such a great question because it balances writing with marketing.

With only one book on the market, readers may not take a chance on your series. Consider that many readers have been burned: they might buy an amazing first book in a series only for the author to die, or worse get bored and move on to another series without writing Book Two. Readers are quite savvy, and some will not invest in a series until it is complete.

To combat this, some writers will write multiple books in the series, say the first three books, or write the entire series and launch the books at the same time or very closely together. Frankly, it's a better experience for readers because if they want the next book, they can buy it right away instead of having to wait months or years.

I don't think there's anything wrong with this method if you can afford it. It's not cheap to write several books without any sales to offset your expenses. But there is a lot of evidence that this method does work.

If you can't do that, then at least make sure that you release your sequels as soon as possible so that Book One doesn't sit on the market for too long without a follow-up.

How long should my series be?

Again: as long as it needs to be! You can write two books or you can write a hundred. It depends entirely on your genre and the enthusiasm of your readers. And your own enthusiasm for the world you've created, of course.

More sales-focused writers might see if sales are dipping from one book to the next. For example, if you're in the middle of a series, and readers aren't buying through to Book Six, then maybe it's time to wrap up the series. But even bestselling series have certain books mid-series that are less popular, so you have to take everything into consideration when making this decision.

How much does it cost to publish my first book and establish my business?

The costs of publishing a book vary wildly, so no answer I give will be one size fits all.

But if you write fiction or nonfiction with no illustrations or special content embedded into the book, you can expect to pay:

- Several hundred to several thousand dollars or pounds for a developmental edit.
- Several hundred to a thousand or more for a copyedit, and about half that for a final proofread.
- Several hundred for a cover design.

These costs vary depending on the work needed on your book, the qualifications of the people you hire, and which services you select. Every author's costs are different.

The costs of establishing your writing business also vary. At a minimum, to create a business entity, you'll pay a minimal fee. A website host and domain name is generally less than $300 per year. Most writing apps are around $50.

There are other costs, to be sure, but it's not expensive to get an author business off the ground.

. . .

Should I write short stories?

Short stories can be a great way for novelists to practice their craft. They can make you money if you submit them to paying magazines and get accepted. Best of all, they're fun and useful gifts for your readers that you can give away or use as a magnet for your mailing list.

So, the answer is yes—if you like short stories, write them to your heart's content, but know how they fit into your publication plan. Short stories don't generally sell well in book format.

What if I have a writing question that's not answered here?

Check the Resources section for more helpful links, and be sure to subscribe to the #AskALLi Member Q&A.

WRITING PRODUCTIVITY

Where and when should I write my book?

The best place to write is wherever you feel the most comfortable. That might be a coffee shop, a park, your couch, or an office in your house with a door.

The best time to write is when you have the most energy. I'm a morning person and do my best work between 5am and 7am. This is also a good time for me because my wife and daughter are asleep.

Find the time where you feel at your best and make that your writing time. Eat right, drink lots of water, and sleep well—that will also boost your energy levels.

How many words should I be writing per day?

I recommend starting small.

How many words per day is normal for you?

Start with 500.

Once you're comfortable with that, try 750.

Go as high as possible until you reach a breaking point. Back down by a few hundred and make that number your writing goal.

As a reference, if you want to write a 50,000-word novel in a month, you would have to write about 1,666 words per day. I've always thought that number was a pretty good word count goal. If you write 50,000 words per month, that would net you 600,000 words, or twelve novels per year. Even if you only achieved half of that number, that would be a major success story in my opinion.

My experience is that writers try to shoot for large daily word counts, but consistency is the real secret. I'd rather write 500 words per day *every day for a year* than have huge word count days with no consistency. As the cliché goes, slow and steady wins the race.

Help! I have writer's block!

The dreaded writer's block happens to the best of us.

I wrote an entire book called *Be a Writing Machine* that is dedicated to helping writers beat writer's block forever, so check it out if you're interested.

Orna has also done much work on all kinds of creative block and recommends practices like F-R-E-E-writing and meditation. Check out her *Creativist Compendium*.

Why do we get writer's block? I believe there are three main reasons:

- Fear.
- Lack of energy and motivation.
- Personal circumstances (illness, deaths in the family, job loss, etc.).

You must deal with fear on your own terms. You have to tame it or dissolve it as much as possible. You can never eliminate fear entirely, but you can learn to write and publish in spite of it.

Remember, you are absolutely good enough to be a writer, no matter what your inner critic says. We all have to start somewhere and we all have to write every day to get better at what we do. That never changes.

Lack of energy and motivation can be fixed by making sure you pick the right projects that you're passionate about, as well as watching what you eat and drink, getting enough sleep, and so on.

I also find that certain parts of books are danger zones for losing energy and motivation, such as the murky middle. You need to develop strategies to deal with these sections, but that's too deep to explore here—I cover this extensively in *Be a Writing Machine.*

And with personal circumstances, things happen. You will get sick, your family members will get sick, and occasionally life will throw you a curveball that you have to deal with. I find that it's hard to write when I'm distracted by personal issues, even if I have the time and energy to write. When I take care of the issue, the writer's block usually goes away.

In any case, writer's block is one of the major problems you will have to learn to cope with early on in your writing journey.

How can I improve my writing speed?

To increase their word counts, some people write sloppier. The idea is to get the words down and worry about them later. That's an easy way to solve this problem, but it'll cause you pain in revision. I don't recommend it.

In my opinion, the best way to increase your writing speed is to find more time to write. If you write 1,000 words per day with an average of two sessions of writing per day, can you find time for a third session? Even if it's only fifteen minutes and you can only write 100 words, you'll increase your daily word count by 10 percent.

I often propose this to writers, and they usually ask "But where can I find that time?"

I'm willing to bet that there are things that you could do less of, like social media or email. The time is there—you just have to find it and be willing to shift priorities.

I'm not saying you need to find hours upon hours. That's not practical. You can improve your writing speed exponentially with just an extra fifteen to twenty minutes per day.

Next, what tools are you using and how skilled are you with them? If you use Microsoft Word, how much of your time is eaten up trying to fix formatting issues? That's precious writing time.

Using a professional writing app and investing in becoming a master at it will pay dividends because you'll be able to use the app to be a better version of yourself. Many writing apps like Scrivener and Ulysses help you get out of your own way so you can focus on the words, which leads us to the next question...

What's the best writing app for writing my book?

I love writing apps. Writing is one of the only creative professions in the world where your primary tool costs less than $100.

There are dozens of different writing apps to help you write virtually anything, so I won't cover all of them. I'll cover the two "tiers" of writing apps with a few notable examples.

The first tier is the free tier. I include Microsoft Word (kind of), Google Docs, and Apple Pages in this tier, as well as open source apps like OpenOffice. They're not specifically designed for writers, but they can get the job done.

The second tier is the paid tier. These apps typically range anywhere from $20 to $75 dollars and are designed exclusively for writers. Scrivener is, in my opinion, the greatest of these apps. I lovingly call it the "caviar" of writing apps. But there's also Ulysses, yWriter, IA Writer, and Byword, to name a few.

These apps offer either a traditional, Microsoft Word-like writing experience, or they use Markdown, which is a stripped-down specialized syntax that uses text files that can be easily converted to any format.

Some features that I think are pretty important for any modern writing app to have are: automatic backups so that you never lose work; a smartphone or tablet edition so you can sync between your desktop and device and work on the go if you desire; the ability to export easily to other formats; and a full-screen mode for distraction-free writing.

There are so many more cool features that writing apps offer, and each one has its own unique flavor.

Almost all of the major writing apps offer trials, so try a few and see which one feels right.

Can dictation help me write faster?

Dictation is the act of speaking into a program that automatically converts your voice to text. You speak twice as fast as you write, so dictation makes a lot of sense, though it has a steep learning curve.

Dictation is also great for writers who have repetitive stress injuries such as carpal tunnel because it involves using your voice, not physical motions, so you can dictate in any position. It's not uncommon to hear writers talk about dictating while lying down or walking in the park, for example.

If you can learn dictation, you can supercharge your word count overnight. Dictation isn't perfect, though, so the end result may be somewhat sloppy.

The time spent cleaning up your manuscript may not be worth it to you unless you learn how to dictate your book with high accuracy, which requires additional learning and skill. I once dictated an entire series with about 92–95 percent accuracy, so it can be done.

At the time of this writing, Dragon by Nuance is the most prominent dictation software. You can dictate at your computer or on the go with its smartphone app. It works great for Windows, but it doesn't work very well for Mac.

Can you truly write books on your phone?

Yes!

Several writing apps have released mobile versions that you can use to write on the go. Assuming you don't suffer from repetitive stress injuries that would prevent you from using these apps, and assuming you don't mind writing with your thumbs, they can be a great way to write more words.

When I switched to Scrivener iOS, I increased my word count by 40 percent. I was surprised how much time I had to write just a few extra words every day. I've used Scrivener iOS to write novels at the grocery store, in the backseat of an Uber, while waiting at the doctor's office, and so much more.

You can also use Bluetooth keyboards with mobile writing apps if you prefer that.

How do I balance writing, publishing, work, and family life?

Few of us start out as full-time writers. It may be necessary to balance writing with your job, family obligations, and work life. The prospect of balancing writing with family alone paralyzes many aspiring writers and prevents them taking the first steps.

It's not easy, but it *is* possible.

First, I would make sure that you have open communication with your spouse or significant other. They are your secret weapon. Be sure to get their support.

At work, if you have the sort of job that requires you bring work home, find ways to be as efficient as possible so that you don't have to take work home with you. If you're constantly bringing work and stress home, find another job that gives you more freedom. This is essential; otherwise, it'll be difficult to balance writing with your job in a healthy way.

I recognize that this advice is not possible for everyone to follow depending on your situation. Your family life, work life, or other obligations may make writing next to impossible.

No one ever said this life was easy. Your family needs will change, you'll go through busy seasons at work, and your writing will make its own demands of you too. The key is to be flexible, and try to develop as much consistency as you can.

How many books should I write at the same time?

I recommend working on one book at a time. You'll accomplish more by focusing on one project until it's finished, then moving on to the next.

How do I know when to abandon my book if it isn't working?

Listen to your intuition. Are you wanting to give up on your book because you are truly at a dead end, or is it because you need more motivation?

Writing a book is hard, especially if it's your first book. It's one of the hardest things you will do, but hard does not mean impossible, and hard does not mean "painful."

Writing a book is hard because it is the spiritual equivalent of looking at yourself in the mirror. Some people don't like what they see; they realize that they don't have the discipline to sit down day after day and write, that they don't have the mental toughness to deal with their inner critic...or that they don't have what it takes, period. Sorry, but it's true.

(And when I say hard, I really mean hard at first. Once you write a few novels, it gets much, much easier. After all, writing should be fun.)

How far along is your book? If you're almost there, keep going. Push yourself. You'll be so glad you did it.

Your gut is your internal compass. It's the quiet voice whispering to you as you look at yourself in the mirror. Chances are, it's telling you to keep going too, but it can be hard to hear it.

Society places so many demands and cultural expectations on us that we can't hear our guts. We're taught that writing is not practical and that we should pursue safer jobs and more interesting hobbies instead. Family and friends may not understand or support our passion for writing. All these things can make it hard to listen to your gut, but with time, you can learn to filter out the noise so you can hear it.

But... after all that harsh talk, if your intuition is still telling you to abandon your work in progress, maybe you should. Put your work away, start a new project as soon as possible (based on what your gut is telling you), and move on.

I've canceled books mid-production before, and honestly, it's painful. But sometimes it *is* the best thing for you.

Listen to your gut, and go where it leads you.

I'm burned out. What do I do?

Burnout is real, and my heart goes out to anyone who experiences it.

By burnout, I'm talking about an existential crisis. It's not writer's block—it's about being so tired of writing that you physically, spiritually, and emotionally cannot bring yourself to do it. Burnout is a mental health issue.

Facing burnout is ultimately about asking yourself two hard questions: what motivates me, and am I on the right path?

I've seen a lot of writers burn out firsthand. It happens for a few reasons. An author can write books in a genre they aren't passionate about, or experience success and then feel chained to that genre to the point where writing feels like "work."

Burnout can happen because an author may not experience any level of meaningful success and therefore finds it difficult to keep going.

Burnout can also happen to the most successful writers. I know one well-known author in particular who burned out because this person got frustrated with other authors attacking the success that the author had built. The attacks were unfounded, by the way. It wore on the author, and they eventually quit because they didn't feel like they deserved that abuse.

So what do you do if burnout happens to you?

First, I'd recommend that you see a licensed therapist. Talk to someone about your feelings. I can't stress this enough. Don't be ashamed to ask for help.

Second, take as much time as you need to rediscover yourself and figure out what drives you.

The writing world is filled with writers who have experienced burnout and bounced back. You *can* bounce back, but take care of yourself and your family first.

What's the best way to deal with rejection?

Just keep going. Rejection doesn't stop coming when you become a published writer.

Readers may not buy your book.

Other authors in your genre won't return your emails.

Literary magazines will reject your short story.

Marketing services will turn you away because your book isn't selling enough for them to promote it.

Readers on your email list won't open your emails, or they'll unsubscribe.

Readers and other authors will give you bad reviews, talk badly about you on forums, and sometimes even send you mean emails, or worse, insult you to your face.

It never stops. Contrary to popular belief, it only gets worse the more successful you become.

Just keep going. I believe in fate; what's meant to happen will happen.

Let me tell you a story unrelated to writing.

I once applied for a job that I really wanted. I wanted it so bad that I was envisioning myself in the role already because it was such a perfect fit for me. My interview went amazingly well, and I thought for sure I'd get the job.

I didn't.

I was crushed. Devastated.

I found out later that the hiring manager was a narcissistic jerk. The person that got the job instead of me ended up leaving the company in disgrace because the manager was impossible to please.

If I had gotten that job, I would have been miserable and it would have dead-ended my career.

I got another job several months later that wasn't nearly as glamorous but opened the door for me to double my salary in just a few years.

Yeah, fate.

Ever since then, I learned to be grateful for the jobs I got, and especially grateful for the jobs I didn't get.

The same is true with rejection.

Be grateful for the times you are accepted, but be especially grateful when someone turns down an opportunity to work with you. Even though it's painful, it's probably for the best.

Rejection still stings nonetheless, but hopefully, that advice gives you some comfort in the hard times.

PART II

EDITORIAL

WHAT IS EDITING?

Editing is the process of turning your raw manuscript into publishable text. It is a stage in both the writing process (rewriting, redrafting, and deepening) and the publishing process (self-editing and professional editing).

It can involve many others as well as yourself.

Before you get into hiring an editor, you have to do a lot of editing as the author, perhaps with the help of a book coach, mentor, other authors, or beta readers.

There are three different stages here and it's important not to confuse them.

1. The deepening and development stage of the writing process (redrafting and rewriting).
2. The correction and clarification stage of the writing process (self-editing).
3. The editing done as part of the publishing process by an editor (professional editing).

ALLIANCE OF INDEPENDENT AUTHORS

Neither rewriting nor self-editing are substitutes for professional editing but they reduce your editorial bill substantially and must be done to satisfaction before an editor will agree to edit your book.

The better a manuscript you can deliver to your editor, the more value you will get from the editorial process.

How long does the editorial process take?

Editing has a number of phases. First you'll self-edit. Then you may use beta readers to give you feedback. Then you bring in the professionals: developmental editors, copyeditors, and proofreaders.

The main thing about the editorial phase is to give it the time and attention it warrants. Every edit is a learning opportunity, and experienced authors welcome that opportunity to improve their book and grow as a writer.

In ALLi's experience, for most writers, getting down the raw first draft takes about one third of the total time needed to have a publishable book. Redrafting and self-editing takes another third of the time, and the final third is spent fixing up problems identified by your editor.

When it comes to hiring the editorial professionals, as with any service for writers, getting on the editor's calendar is half the struggle. Good editors are booked up months in advance.

Once your editor begins working on the book, it takes at least a couple of days to review it. A full developmental edit will take longer than a proofreading, and in some cases can take several weeks or months, and maybe even more than one pass to get your books to publishable standard.

Do I REALLY need an editor?

Yes. Even the best authors make bad editors of their own work. Sorry.

You're too close to your book, so you can't view it objectively. An objective third party will help you develop a better manuscript. It does involve a cost, but it's better than putting a subpar book on the market. At ALLi, we always say the best marketing is good editing.

SELF-EDITING AND BETA READERS

REWRITING AND REDRAFTING

What's the difference between rewriting and self-editing?

You don't start self-editing as soon as you've typed "The End" for the first time. Unless you're an experienced author who writes to plan, the very first draft of your book is likely to be rough and raw. As part of the writing process, you'll redraft and revise and rewrite, adding in more text over here, while stripping it out over there.

Most emerging authors do quite a bit of rewriting before they have a final draft. Final draft comes when an author honestly feels there is nothing else they can do to improve the book. They then put the manuscript away with the intention of starting the self-editing process once some time has elapsed.

More experienced authors can write their books in one draft, eschewing rewriting altogether. This means getting it right in your head first, which is such a daunting task for some authors that it puts them right off. But there is no doubt that it is a quicker and cleaner process.

Over time some authors clean their process up so they can write in this way. Others remain a "shitty first draft" writer forever. So long as the books are being produced, it doesn't matter. The important point here is that self-editing should not begin until the rewriting is done. You need to wear a different hat when you're creating than when you're correcting.

The more you separate those two functions, the quicker your book will progress. Your goal with self-editing should be to *refine*, not *rewrite*.

How do I know if I need another rewrite?

Leave it for a while. Lock it away. Forget about it. Go write something else. Come back after a while and see what you find.

Do remember the law of diminishing returns—if you believe in rewriting, there will come a point where rewriting too much can actually start to hurt your story.

I thought the book was finished, but now I fear it isn't!

This happens, particularly with new writers. All authors want their first draft to be their final draft. In practice, the process is often messier and more challenging than that, especially at the start.

If you're a new author, you may well discover real problems with your book when you self-edit. That chapter you wrote that felt amazing will suddenly look like crap. The tendency at this point is to rewrite.

Don't be disheartened. Know that the iterative process is essential to making your book all it can be. Also understand that what you're learning from any rewriting or self-editing will help you with your next book. The experience you gain from writing more books means you're better able to identify mistakes in the process. But the only way you can do this is to *write more books*.

Be flexible and responsive, aiming always to separate writing and rewriting from self-editing. Also consider that whatever flaws you think exist in the manuscript, your readers may not see it that way. They may actually enjoy that chapter you think is crap.

This is why I personally believe you should keep rewriting to a minimum.

I published my book but I'm not happy with it. Should I rewrite?

I've learned many things in my time as a writer, but few are as important as this fact: a writer is always the worst judge of their work. Always.

Yes, the pain we feel when we look at our finished work is real, but that doesn't mean the work has real problems. We must ask: how much of this is about us and how much is about the reader?

How much are you selling? What are your reviews saying? These are the real questions to ask, not "Is this any good?" or "Am I happy with this?"

I can't tell you whether you should rewrite your book. I *can* tell you this, though: I know writers who rewrite their books endlessly, never to finish them because the books are never "good enough." Don't be one of those writers.

Should I get a writing coach?

If you can afford it and if you want to break through to the next level as a writer, or move past barriers that are getting in the way of your success, or if you need help emotionally to transform the process of writing from stressful to joyful, then the *right* writing coach can certainly help. Coaches are not essential, however. If you're a self-starter, you can also learn from blogs, books, and other resources.

SELF-EDITING

· · ·

I don't have enough money for an editor. Can't I just self-edit?

Redrafting and self-editing are essential parts of the writing process, but you've got to hand the book over to the professionals. In Orna's opinion, going over and over a manuscript in the effort to avoid hiring an editor is a waste of valuable writing time and can actually be a sophisticated form of creative resistance, stopping you from moving through the publication of the current book and onto the next. Beg, borrow, or steal the money you need for an editor.

How can I learn to self-edit better?

You need to become objective about the book that you've just spent months passionately writing. There are four tried-and-tested ways to do this: time, place, format, and audio.

Time. Time is the most important. When you've finished your final draft, you must put time between you and the book before you begin to self-edit. In Orna's opinion, some months is recommended, and the ideal is to put your final draft away and begin a new book, or return to edit a previous final draft manuscript. Working on another book gives you time to grow as a writer before you return to self-editing. You will have become detached. The more complex and literary your book, the longer you should leave between drafts.

In my opinion (which I confess is the opposite of Orna's and a bit radical), a few days or a week or two is enough time. Write the book, and then spend some time working on your author business during the meantime, like fixing things on your website or doing some basic marketing. Set a deadline, and once it comes, start self-editing. Rip the bandage off. If waiting up to a year between writing and self-editing suits your goals, that's fine, but it won't if you are impatient to publish.

At the end of the day, you've heard both sides. Do what is best for you.

Place. You need to wear a different hat when you're editing than when you're writing. To help yourself to develop that, edit somewhere different from where you write. Go on a retreat. Take the manuscript on holiday. If you write at home, edit in a café—or vice versa. Use the local library. Or simply a different room in your house. Think creatively about where you might get a different perspective.

Format. Seeing your work in a different layout or font, such as on a different screen or in hard copy, moves the mind a step away from the original work. If you wrote your book on a computer, read it on an iPad or phone—or vice versa. Many self-publishing authors begin their self-editing with a print proof of the book from Amazon or IngramSpark. Highlight and make notes on your different format, then return to the computer with a list of what you need to do.

Audio. Audio is a formatting option that deserves special mention. Hearing your book read back, text-to-speech, is free and can make poor sentence construction, incorrect word usage, or missing words very obvious. Be aware that it may not catch missing or incorrect punctuation though.

Reading your work aloud is also helpful, though reading your whole book aloud can be tedious. Try reading the first few chapters, a few in the middle, and your last few chapters aloud. It works wonders.

You will also learn from how your professional editor works. Many US-based editors use the *Chicago Manual of Style*, so you could learn the basics of that manual and incorporate them into your self-editing. If you're writing in British English, do the same with *New Oxford Style Manual*. But remember these are preferences, not rules.

Once you work with an editor for the first time, I recommend you also keep track of the areas where the editor has to keep correcting you. Maybe you always get semicolons wrong, or you're wordy when you describe a new character for the first time. Understanding potential weak areas as you write them will help you create cleaner manuscripts in the future.

And of course, I recommend consuming blogs, books, videos, podcasts, and other resources on self-editing, as they can help you improve your skill level.

· · ·

Are apps like Grammarly and ProWritingAid worth it?

Grammarly and ProWritingAid are advanced grammar and spellcheckers. They are the two most popular, but there are many more. Advanced spellcheckers are light-years better than the spelling and grammar programs built in to your computer, and they can help you catch more typos. While they are not a substitute for an editor, they can serve as a last line of defense after your book has been edited.

I recommend testing a few different apps to see which one is more accurate for your writing style. In my personal experience, I find that Grammarly is better for nonfiction and ProWritingAid is better for fiction.

BETA READERS

What are beta readers?

Beta readers are volunteers who agree to read your book and offer feedback.

Beta reading happens when you feel like you've done as much self-editing as you possibly can. You then send it to beta readers for feedback.

Beta readers offer you their comments, observations, and suggestions for improvement of your manuscript prior to publication, *before* sending it to your professional editor.

Ideal beta readers can be trusted authors, recruited readers, family, or friends. The first qualification is that they are well-read in your genre (not much point giving your YA lesbian mermaid romance to a space opera fan) and the second qualification is that they'll give you an honest assessment.

In my personal opinion (and experience), the best beta reader is someone who is *not* a family member or a friend. Bless your family and friends, but they don't have the objectivity that you need.

. . .

Should I use beta readers?

That's up to you. Some authors swear by them, others prefer to work alone until they pass the work to a professional editor. The best way to find out is to try it.

What should I look for in a beta reader?

Honesty, above all. Don't recruit anyone who will be overly nice and positive for fear of hurting your feelings. This isn't about self-aggrandizement or creating an echo chamber—it's about honest feedback.

You want articulate people who can convey what they think clearly, but who aren't prescriptive. A beta reader who claims that all the major characters have to be introduced in the first chapter, or that a chapter should always begin with a summary of what happened in the last, is an opinionated person who is fonder of their own theories than of your book.

You also want to focus on developmental, structural, or substantive editing (see the next section, Working with Editors, for more on this). You're looking for feedback about big issues—plot, character, pacing, and voice in fiction; argument, structure, and voice in nonfiction—not detailed issues of word choice or sentence structure.

How many beta readers do I need?

Three is the magic number, but I wouldn't do more than five. The wider the range of opinions you receive, the better, so think about the quality and mix, as well as the quantity of your beta readers.

Where do I find beta readers?

You can search online for "find beta readers" and see what comes up. Increasingly, there are readers who offer paid beta reader services. There are also Facebook and Goodreads for beta reader groups, but make sure to read the group rules and follow them to the letter. You can also reach out to author friends.

Treat your beta readers well, and remember: they're volunteering their time to help you. Expect delays, and, moreover, expect some readers not to follow through with their promise. Having a couple of betas will insulate you against this risk.

WORKING WITH PROFESSIONAL EDITORS

I don't understand the different kinds of editing and which one I need.

Let's go over the different types of editing.

Developmental editing looks at your story at a big-picture level. A developmental editor looks at your story structure, your character development, and the overall feel of your story. The edits they recommend will almost always involve rewriting, restructuring, or expanding on what you've already written. Generally speaking, a developmental editor is not going to point out many typos or grammar errors.

Developmental editing is the most expensive editing you can buy, and it can cost anywhere from several hundred to several thousand dollars because of the time involved. Developmental editing is also known as content editing or substantive editing.

In Orna's opinion, if you have a complex book, or if you have any doubts that you might have left some parts undeveloped, or if you don't have a firm understanding of writing craft, it's very likely that you need a developmental edit. Yes, the money spent on a developmental editor would go a long way in another area of your writing business, but it's worth bearing in mind that every traditional publisher considers a developmental edit to be a worthwhile investment, so it's likely to be the same for you.

If you choose a developmental editor, be sure to check if that person is in ALLi's Service Ratings Directory. Developmental editing is an area where writers can get frequently scammed. There are decent developmental editors on the market, though it may take research to find one that's right for your needs.

Copyediting is the bread and butter of editing. A copyeditor reviews your work word by word for meaning at the paragraph and sentence level. The good copyeditors will comment on your story and whether a particular scene works. Primarily, though, a copyeditor is interested in making sure the story flows, that the words on the page are the right ones, and that there are as few typos as possible. Copyediting is significantly less expensive than developmental editing, and in my humble opinion, if you can only afford one editor, I'd hire a copyeditor. Copyediting is where the book starts to come alive.

Proofreading is the last line of defense. A proofreader reads the book in its final format for typos, remaining crucial errors and layout problems. If you hired a copyeditor, the proofreader is essentially checking that editor's work, not doing the major tasks of editing. For this reason, proofreading is the cheapest type of editing you can buy because it takes less time.

My personal publishing process is to hire a copyeditor and proofreader, and I'd make sure they were two different people. This way, when you're done with your book, you can rest easy knowing that it's as clean as can be.

If I can only afford one editor, who should I choose: developmental editor, copyeditor, or proofreader?

Developmental editors are expensive and are not necessary for every single book. You probably don't need developmental editing for a short story or a straightforward nonfiction book, for example. Most authors choose to hire a developmental editor at the beginning of their writing journeys, but that's also the time when they have the least amount of money to invest.

In my opinion, a copyedit is the one type of edit I would not do without. If money were an issue, I wouldn't let a book go to market without at least a proofread.

Where can I find an editor?

As with any service, I would make ALLi's Service Ratings Directory your first port of call.

If that fails, ask writers in your genre who they use for editing. It helps to hire someone familiar with your genre.

If that fails, I would use a freelancer site like Upwork, an agency site like Reedsy, or the free directories of nonprofit professional associations for editors, such as the American Copy Editors Society in the US or the Chartered Institute of Editing and Proofreading in the UK.

Using those methods, you should be able to find an editor who suits your needs quickly.

How do I choose the best editor?

Experience is important. I always recommend an editor who has edited a lot of books in your genre if possible. At a minimum, you want to hire a fiction editor for fiction and a nonfiction editor for nonfiction. If you hire an editor who is really good at memoirs to edit your mystery novel... well, it probably won't go very well.

The best editors are partners with you in the creative process. They correct you, challenge you, and push you to think differently in a way that serves your story and your readers. That's why having experience in your genre and subgenre (if possible) is important.

. . .

What's the best way of working with an editor?

Ask the editor what they want and how you can make the process easier.

An industry-standard tip is to provide your editor with a style sheet. A style sheet lists all of the proper nouns in your story so that the editor knows how character names, places, and special words should be spelled. It may also include some usage items, like how to deal with numbers—do you spell them out or use numerals?

Check the Resources section for some great links to help you develop a style sheet that will make you look like a rock star.

Some more things you can do to make your editor's job easier: ask them any questions you might have as a comment in your manuscript so they can answer it in their report; provide any other helpful information that will help them keep all the details in your book straight; and prioritize their emails if they have questions.

Is it OK if my editor is also an author?

Like I said, authors make bad editors. The exception is if the author in question has made a professional career of editing, has the relevant training by editing an extensive amount of books. Then they may be a good fit for your book.

What does an editor cost?

It depends on your book's length, but expect to pay several hundred to several thousand dollars for a developmental edit, several hundred for a copyedit, and about half that for a proofread.

What if I hire a bad editor?

At ALLi, we regularly receive questions from new members who hired a bad editor.

Imagine this: you hire an editor, and instead of reinforcing your book, they butcher it. They recommend grammatically incorrect changes, miss tons of typos, make bad comments that don't do your book justice, and more.

Then they hand you the book, take your money, and you're left holding a manuscript that's worse than when you started.

It can happen, especially if you don't vet your editor.

Generally, editors do a good job. You'll have a certain feeling of euphoria when you're done working through an editor's edits. If you know what that feels like, then you'll know immediately if an editor has let you down.

If you find yourself in this situation, take a deep breath.

The best course of action is to start over with a new editor. If the former editor did more bad than good, maybe you start from scratch and send the new editor your unedited manuscript. Or maybe you can try to salvage what the former editor did. However you choose to proceed, it's an expensive and an energy-exhausting predicament. But you can overcome it and you *can* get your book ready for publication.

My editor doesn't do sample edits. Should I walk away?

Sample edits are a great way to gauge whether an editor is a good fit for your book. It usually involves the editor editing a few pages for free, fixing typos, and making general comments. However, some editors don't do sample edits because they're giving away their work for free, especially if the writer doesn't choose their services.

What you may see instead is that the editor will charge a small fee for a sample edit, and if you choose their services, they will subtract that fee from the total cost of the editing. I think this is fair. If an editor doesn't offer sample edits at all, I recommend proposing this alternative so you can at least get an idea of what the editor is like. If the editor refuses and asks you to pay blindly for their services, I would walk away.

Sample edits are more common with developmental and copyeditors and less common with proofreaders, though still recommended.

My editor is no longer available mid-series. What are my options?

This is a terrible situation to be in.

Editors enter and exit the business all the time for many reasons. They may also raise their rates to a cost that is not affordable for you.

Let's say that you have a five-book series, and your editor isn't available after Book Three. You have two books left. Your previous editor knew your story world very well, and now you have to start over with someone new.

Here's what I would do: I would find an editor who had availability to work on a large project. Explain the situation to them, and offer to pay them to *proofread* Books One through Three, and then *copyedit* the rest of the series moving forward.

It'll be expensive, but this will at least ensure that your new editor is up to speed with your universe. They'll hopefully also catch a few more errors that the last editor missed. If that's too expensive, negotiate to see what you can get. Some editors may offer you a discount if you bring them multiple books at the same time, for example.

What if I don't agree with my editor's edits?

Ultimately, it's your book and you don't have to do anything an editor says. But you *do* want someone whose advice you can trust, which is why hiring the right people is so important.

You won't always like an editor's edits, and that's OK. The editing process can be uncomfortable. Editors can come up with solutions that don't work as far as the author is concerned.

Usually, though, if they raise something, you should consider what's being said. You may not like the recommendation and you may not accept it, but it may help you think about a better solution.

If you find yourself disagreeing with *everything* an editor recommends, then you either hired the wrong person or you can't take criticism. Feedback can be difficult sometimes.

Never take it personally, and never get personal about it. The editor is expressing an opinion about your book, not about you. (If your editor *is* making things personal, well… that's another story entirely.)

Absorbing and responding positively to constructive editorial feedback is a key skill that every successful author has developed.

PART III

BOOK DESIGN AND FORMATTING

COVER DESIGN

What defines a good book cover?

Let's face it: as much as we try to live up to the mantra "don't judge a book by its cover," we do. Readers *definitely* judge books by their covers.

It's clear that a book cover has a major impact on sales and can determine a book's fate. Less clear, though, is what constitutes a good book cover. Every genre is different, every reader is different, and every writer's circumstances are different.

Go to any online retailer and you will see books with terrible covers that are bestsellers and books with amazing covers that don't sell. It's especially frustrating to be in the latter camp.

Here's what I've learned over the years after working with designers on over sixty book covers:

- It's impossible to know if a cover will sell your book until you publish.
- The books that do best tend to look similar to other books in their immediate genre and niche.

- Book covers tend to work best when they are billboards rather than works of art. In other words, the cover should exist to show readers what the book's genre and subgenre are rather than the story inside.
- Simple is almost always better.

We could discuss color choice, contrast, composition, typography, and other design elements, but I have yet to see any conclusive evidence that having a certain design element on your cover will help you sell more books.

To give yourself the best possible chance of designing an effective cover, my advice is to find a competent designer with experience in your genre and see how readers respond. Over time, you'll learn what works for your readership.

A book cover only has five major elements:

- Title
- Subtitle, tagline, series statement, or testimonial/blurb
- Author name
- Foreground
- Background

If you understand this breakdown, then you can be more intentional about what you want your cover to look like, and you can make informed decisions based on other books in your genre. Maybe all of the covers in your genre have a certain type of background (like urban fantasy having a city in the background, for example, or space opera having spaceships). If you figure out what commonalities the comparable books in your genre have for each cover element, you can move closer to what the "picture of good" looks like in your genre. Just understand that this picture, however, is a moving target that changes as the years go by.

WORKING WITH A DESIGNER

. . .

What's the process of working with a cover designer?

The book cover design process has several steps:

- You communicate your needs to the designer.
- The designer locates material to use on the cover (they may involve you in this process, or they may not).
- The designer provides you with a first draft. If the designer is illustrating the cover, the draft may be in black and white or grayscale; the designer will colorize the design once you approve it.
- You provide feedback and the designer makes updates until you are satisfied or you exhaust the amount of revisions the designer allows.
- The designer delivers the final product.

Overall, the process is straightforward.

How long does the cover design process take?

It depends on the designer. The biggest consideration to think about is the designer's calendar. The good designers are usually booked several months in advance, sometimes more. I have a designer who books eight months in advance, and I know of designers that have waiting lists of eighteen months or more. Not kidding!

When the designer starts working on your design, however, you can expect to wait a few days or weeks to receive your first draft.

Once you receive your first draft and you provide feedback, most designers will turn around revisions in a few days, usually sooner. The entire process takes a few weeks on average, and much less if your book is a sequel in an existing series that the designer is already familiar with.

Now that we've discussed the timelines, there's another important question you need to ask...

Should I design my book cover before or after I finish writing?

Writers fall into two camps. The first camp prefers to design the cover before they start writing or while they are working on the manuscript. For these writers, the cover inspires the story.

The second camp prefers to design the cover after the book is finished, mostly because they don't know what the book will be about. Also, if you design a cover before you start writing and the story changes significantly, then you may have to redesign the cover.

I've done both, and I don't have a preference. It depends on the project and how confident I am that the cover *won't* change when I'm done with the manuscript.

Whatever you do, make sure you get on your cover designer's calendar so you don't create delays in publishing your book!

Where do I find a cover designer?

I recommend that you start with ALLi's Service Ratings Directory as your first port of call. ALLi's Watchdog Desk reviews service providers for writers and rates them based on whether they meet our Code of Standards. If they don't, we'll tell you, and why. With this directory, you can rest assured that the designer you pick will treat you fairly and do their best to provide you a good product.

I also recommend looking for designers that have experience in your genre. The best way to do this is to look at other self-published books in your genre that are selling well and that have decent reviews. Open the e-book sample and look for a designer name on the copyright page. That's typically where authors put cover credits. Find a designer whose style you like and see if they are available.

If that fails, you can find good designers on freelancer sites like Upwork or Reedsy. You can post a job and invite designers to come to you, or you can request free quotes from qualified designers who might be a good fit for you. Make sure to review their portfolio to see if their design style aligns with your book, and also make sure that the designer has a track record of customer satisfaction.

If you find a designer who isn't listed in ALLi's Service Ratings Directory, contact our Watchdog and they will investigate them for future writers who work with that designer.

What if I can't pick just one designer? Is crowdsourcing my book cover more effective?

There are websites that allow you to get design proposals from many designers at the same time. This is called crowdsourcing. You pay for the design you like best. At the time of this writing, 99designs is the most popular of these crowdsourcing sites.

I've talked to several authors who like crowdsourcing because it gives them options, usually at the same price you would pay a single designer.

You'll have to gauge the quality of the designers and their work product to see if this method is right for you, as it is not for everyone.

What about premade book covers?

Many designers design premade book covers and sell them for a small fee. When you buy one, you provide your book details and the designer puts them on the cover and removes it from sale. You walk away with an original book cover at a fraction of the cost.

The quality of premade covers varies. Some are poor, but some are very good.

Premades are a respectable choice for an author on a budget, but there are a few things you need to think about:

- Is your book in a series? If so, does the designer offer enough options to complete your series, or will you have to pay them to create extra designs? If you have to pay them to design something original in addition to the premade, it's probably cheaper to pay for an original cover design that fits your book to begin with.
- Premades are generally cost-effective alternatives for standalone books, or for authors who only plan to publish a handful of books in their lifetime.
- If you plan on writing a lot of books, you'll have a tough time making cohesive author branding for your covers if you use premades. You may have to pay to rebrand premade covers in the future, which will likely be more expensive than hiring a designer upfront.
- Premades aren't designed for your book, and it's difficult to find one that might match the spirit of what you're trying to achieve.

I'm not knocking premades. My first few covers were premades because it was all I could afford. I paid a lot of money to rebrand my covers several years later. It was an expensive lesson for me.

Just understand that you're accepting some major future downsides if you decide to buy premades.

I've heard that there are good designers on Fiverr.com. Can I find a designer there?

Fiverr is a platform where you can hire people to do one-off tasks for a flat fee. Services used to start at five dollars, hence the name of the platform, but overall prices have increased somewhat since then.

My opinion: avoid Fiverr *for book covers*. I don't dislike Fiverr; I actually think the platform is great and I use it a lot for a number of services. It's just a bad place to buy a book cover unless you supply your designer with the stock images and fonts, which kind of defeats the purpose.

When you pay rock-bottom prices for a cover design, you tend to get what you pay for.

There are a lot of designers on Fiverr who do not have a track record of success. Worse, it's not uncommon to see designers there showcasing book covers *they didn't design* as a marketing tool to attract customers. I've seen it firsthand. That's not Fiverr's fault, because this kind of thing is difficult to police, but it *is* a problem for you.

And if that weren't enough, there's no guarantee that your designer there will have the necessary licenses to use the images they incorporate into your cover. If a designer were to use a copyrighted image without the owner's consent on *your book cover*, who do you think is going to get a legal demand letter first?

Exactly. You.

To be fair, this is an exposure you could have with any designer, but at the time of this writing, the issue seems to be especially prevalent on Fiverr.

That leads us to another interesting question…

Do I need a contract with my cover designer?

Contracts are almost unheard of with cover designers. It's customary to pay for the service and be done. However, a short contract may help eliminate confusion and protect both parties.

For example, you may want to have your cover designer sign an agreement that they will secure the proper license to any content they don't own that is incorporated into your cover. This way, you minimize your chances of a designer downloading and using photos they don't have permission to use.

It may also be helpful to specify in the contract that the designer will hold you harmless for any claims of copyright infringement arising from the cover.

Again, contracts are not typically customary or required, but they are a smart idea. At a minimum, I would at least ask your cover designer where they get their images from and what type of licenses they secure, as well as a list of fonts used on the cover. You can then research what type of license is required and ask the appropriate follow-up questions to protect yourself.

For example, if a designer gets their photos from a stock photo site, I'll look at the license agreement on that site. There may be hidden obligations in that license that YOU have to abide by, which leads us to the next question…

Am I limited to how many books I can sell before having to pay my designer again?

Reputable designers charge a one-time flat fee and won't ask for more money if a book is successful.

However, the content they incorporate into your cover may place restrictions on the number of books you can sell before having to upgrade your license.

For example, Shutterstock.com sells a standard license for its stock images that implies unlimited use for e-books but states that you can only sell up to 500,000 physical products under that license. That applies to paperbacks, hardcovers, bookmarks, and merchandise, just to name a few things that you might do with your cover. If you sell more than 500,000 physical products, you would need to upgrade to Shutterstock's Enhanced License, which is significantly more expensive.

If your designer uses Shutterstock, you would need to know these license terms because your designer can't track your sales. Knowing the terms keeps everyone safe.

Not all content sites are created equal, so it pays to understand the licenses your designer is securing. It's more work for you, but you'll sleep better at night.

. . .

What should I expect to pay for a cover design?

The cost of book cover design varies wildly, but expect to pay at least several hundred dollars or pounds.

More established cover designers will charge more, and less experienced cover designers will charge less.

Just because a designer costs more doesn't necessarily mean that you will receive a better design. Ask other writers in your genre what they typically pay.

What information does a designer need?

Most designers will ask you to fill out a questionnaire. The information needed might include:

- Title.
- Subtitle, series statement, tagline, endorsement or blurb.
- Author name.
- Genre/subgenre.
- Synopsis (1–2 paragraphs).
- A sample chapter or the entire manuscript.
- Important places, objects, or symbols in the book.
- Descriptions of your main character (if fiction).
- Color preferences.
- Which retailers you are publishing the book on.
- Paperback and hardcover details (trim size, page color, etc.).
- Similar books in your genre (some designers won't design a book cover without this).

My advice is to be clear and concise. Don't give your designer pages and pages of descriptions or you'll confuse them. A confused designer will deliver a confused design, which will confuse readers on what your book is about.

It's also important not to micromanage your designer. If you control the design too much, you also run the risk of confusing readers.

Pick the right designer, give them a clear vision, and let them do what they do best.

Your number one goal when working with a designer is to provide clarity: clarity on who your ideal readers are and the high-level concepts of your book.

How can I build a good relationship with my designer?

I recommend asking your designer what you can do for them. They will appreciate that.

Here are some practical ideas to build a good rapport with your designer:

- Be respectful of their calendar and give them enough lead time to start working on your project.
- Provide them a clear and concise vision of what you want on your cover (but you knew I was going to say that).
- Create a Pinterest board with similar books in your genre and send that to your designer with your questionnaire. I do this with my designers, and every single one has thanked me for doing it.
- Be open and honest with them about what you're looking for. If there's something you don't like, tell them—but more importantly, tell them why and give them a chance to fix it. Your designer wants to make you happy.
- Don't be a jerk.
- Don't be "that" client—the one who nitpicks every little thing or asks for 1,000 revisions.
- When providing feedback about what you want them to change, use bullet points, not paragraphs. It sounds silly, but it makes it easier for the designer because it gives them clear direction.
- Prioritize their emails and respond to them promptly.
- Thank them and show gratitude! If your book succeeds, your designer will have played a major part. One of the

best ways to thank your designer is to send them a referral.

Follow this advice and you'll find that your designer will look forward to working with you, and they may even go the extra mile on your next project. They may even start working on your next book sooner than you expected.

Who owns the copyright to my cover?

Based on what we've discussed so far, a cover consists of many copyrighted elements. Generally speaking, your designer owns the copyright to your cover design unless you have a contract that specifies otherwise.

The designer grants you a license to use the content for your book cover (and marketing materials). Typically, it is unwise to make any changes to your cover without your designer's consent. Always ask for permission if you need to make a change. The designer will usually be happy to make it for you, either for free or for a small charge.

Also, if you use the book cover for a product not originally discussed with your designer, always ask for permission. For example, if you create merchandise or physical banners with your book on it, let your designer know. They usually won't mind, but there may be a license impact that you need to be aware of.

Also, you retain the copyright to the written content in your book, and your designer doesn't own any part of it... unless you sign a contract that says otherwise, and I don't recommend that!

How and where should I credit my designer?

Most designers will ask for credit with a link to their website on the copyright or acknowledgments pages of your book. Others may ask if they can put their name and logo on the back cover. These options are all industry standard.

The issue is when certain designers ask you to include them in the byline on the sales page of your book, so that their name appears next to yours. These designers rely on discoverability through the success of the books they create.

My experience is that reputable designers will not ask you to share credit on the book sales page. You performed the hard work of writing the book. Does it make sense to share a byline with someone who didn't contribute blood, sweat, and tears to the project?

My opinion is no. You're the creative director of your business. Don't give your power away.

The notable exception is illustrators who create illustrations that become part of the story. That is an example where including your designer in the byline makes sense.

Should I use a subtitle, tagline, series statement, or an endorsement on my cover?

First off, what are all of those things?

A *subtitle* is typically used in nonfiction to demonstrate value. For example, one of my books is called *Be a Writing Machine*. The subtitle is "Write Faster and Smarter, Beat Writer's Block, and Be Prolific." The subtitle promises what the book will deliver.

A *tagline* is used in fiction to tease the story. A tagline serves a similar function to a movie poster—it drums up intrigue. For example, I have a fantasy novel called *Old Dark*, and it's about a blood-thirsty dragon lord who is thousands of years old. The tagline on the first edition of the book was "You're never too old to rule the world."

A *series statement* is primarily used with fiction series, and it tells the reader which book they're looking at. For example, my dragon book would say "The Last Dragon Lord: Book One."

An *endorsement* (also known as a blurb) can be used in fiction or nonfiction, and it's usually a brief statement from another author or a famous person saying something nice about the book or the author. The great thing about endorsements is that they can be used on the back cover of the book as well.

Which one should you use?

It depends. Look at what the other books in your subgenre are doing, and do that.

If you think about your cover as a marketing tool, here are my opinions (and my opinions only).

If you write nonfiction, where the goal is to educate your readers (like this book is doing), your safest bet is almost always a subtitle. A smart subtitle tells readers what they are going to get, which will influence their buying decision. If you have connections and can get a successful author, influencer, or celebrity *in your niche* to endorse your book, and an endorsement would make readers pay attention, then an endorsement could work for you, but *only* if the person giving the endorsement is a true heavyweight. For example, if you write a book about entrepreneurship and get Richard Branson to endorse it, then be prepared to make some serious cash. A local entrepreneur who is unknown outside of your city? Not so much.

Remember that you can also put the endorsement on the back cover. Some nonfiction authors put multiple endorsements on the back cover. Traditional publishers sometimes do this too.

For educational nonfiction, a series statement is OK as well, but a well-crafted subtitle will usually outperform it every time.

If you write nonfiction whose primary goal is to entertain, then a subtitle or tagline will tell the audience what to expect.

If you write standalone fiction that is not part of a series, a tagline or an endorsement is probably your best option because you want to hook readers with something quick.

If you write series fiction, a series statement is probably your best option. Sure, it's boring, but you would be surprised how often readers get confused about which book in a series they should read next. Make it easy for them.

Again, these are my opinions only, but I hope they give you some ideas to consider. Every book is different, so do what you think is best.

You have options and flexibility. Your designer can easily change a tagline to a series statement, for example.

Pro tip: when you finalize your cover, ask the designer to provide you with different options, such as one version with a series statement and another version with a tagline. You can then test them out to see which one works best. It'll usually cost nothing for your designer to create alternate versions when you're in the design process. If you ask them long after the design is complete, they may charge you.

Should my cover have a person on it?

It depends on your genre. More specifically, your *subgenre.*

For example, most subgenres of science fiction tend to have at least one person on the cover. However, space opera is a notable exception—it's not uncommon to see spaceships as the main subject on the cover.

In the mystery genre, it would be unusual to put a character on the cover of a detective novel, unless it was also in a subgenre of science fiction or fantasy. Pure detective novel covers usually don't feature a character—if they do, it's a silhouette or a shape. Cozy mysteries don't typically have characters on them either.

I'm making generalizations, of course, but hopefully this illustrates how subgenres differ wildly within the same genre. Reader tastes and preferences change over time, so you have to consider that too. Narrowing your research down to recently published books in your genre will also help you make more accurate decisions. My definition of recent is four years—any older than that and you risk basing your decisions on a cover that might be outdated. That's a personal opinion, though.

The answer is to study the books in your genre and align your cover with reader expectations. This will make it easier for you to sell more books.

Should I go with stock photos or original material on my cover?

If you opt for a cover with a character on it, you have three choices: a stock photography model, a model from a unique photo shoot that is specific to your book and no one else's, or an illustration. Each has their pros and cons, and a designer will typically specialize in only one style.

Stock photos are the easiest to find, and designers buy them from sites like Shutterstock or Getty Images. The pros of stock images are that they're cheap and it's easy to find any kind of model you're looking for. Skilled designers can use photo manipulation techniques to make a common stock photo model look original, like taking the head of one model and putting it on the body of another. The con of stock photos is that other people can use the same model on their book covers. Though rare in the same subgenre, it can happen.

A unique photo shoot ensures that no one will use the same model, but… who's going to do the photo shoot? You? Your designer? Or will you have to hire a photographer? Where will you shoot? How will you find a model? What will they wear? This option is expensive and a challenge to coordinate.

Illustrations these days can be so photo-realistic, you don't know you're looking at an illustration. Skilled designers can paint incredibly life-like characters. The pro is that you'll receive an original design, but the con is that illustrated covers are more expensive.

Again, it goes back to the holy grail of this chapter—do what others in your subgenre are doing. If all the bestselling books in your genre are illustrated, try to get an illustrated cover if you can afford it. If all you can afford is stock photography, there's no shame in that.

· · ·

What about Creative Commons images?

Some photographers make their photos available via a Creative Commons license, and there are search engines such as the Creative Commons Search where you can find images that are in the public domain or that you can use for free commercially.

My opinion is to avoid Creative Commons images on your cover for one major reason.

Occasionally, someone who doesn't own the copyright to an image may upload it to another website and claim it as their own under a Creative Commons license. You may not know about the copyright infringement until you receive a cease and desist letter. You don't want to put yourself in that position.

However, if you *do* use a Creative Commons image, be certain that you have the correct license and follow the Creative Commons license requirements to the letter. At a minimum, this means giving the creator an attribution. Whatever you do, never use an image that is contrary to how the creator intended (i.e. don't use an image licensed for personal use for commercial use). This will keep you out of trouble.

My designer sent me the first draft of my design and I HATE it. What now?

The honest truth is that, out of the many covers I've had designed so far, only a few first draft designs satisfied my expectations.

Though strange to say, it's normal for a first draft to miss the mark.

With leadership on your part and responsiveness from your designer, you can easily fix the problem. Out of sixty-ish cover designs, I've always walked away feeling good about the end result.

If you don't like your cover, here's what I would do: first, take a deep breath, and then find something else to do for at least fifteen minutes. Let your mind process why you don't like the design.

When you've had time to process it, draft up a response and use this format:

Dear [Cover Designer],

Thank you for the design. Here are my thoughts.

What I like:

- xxx
- xx

What I would like to change:

- xxx
- xxx

Title:

- xxx

Subtitle:

- xxx

Author Name:

- xxx

Foreground:

- xxx

Background:

- xxx

Element by element, tell them what works and what doesn't. Use bullet points.

You'll have a better chance at fixing the design if you approach it with a cool, logical head.

Also, it could be that the reason the design doesn't work is because one or two of the elements are off. If you fix them, maybe the design will be great.

Often, I find that small changes make big differences.

The only real showstopper on a cover is the model. If the model isn't right, then it will impact everything else. If there's a problem with the model, fix that first.

Experiencing a poor first design is not insurmountable. You can overcome it!

My cover design isn't working out, even after several rounds of feedback.

Even after a good-faith effort on both sides, it's possible that your cover might not work out. It happens.

Have an honest conversation with your designer about what you're feeling. If they ask for a final opportunity to make you happy, give it to them. And if it still doesn't work out, negotiate a payment arrangement and the best way for both of you to walk away cleanly. Chances are your designer has other projects they need to work on and it's in their best interests to walk away too.

Make sure you understand the designer's process for canceling a cover *before* you get into an agreement with them.

· · ·

Help! My designer is no longer in the business and I'm in the middle of a series.

This is an unenviable situation to be in, but it can happen. Designers are human; they may quit to pursue other opportunities or deal with personal issues, pass away, or become another author's or publisher's exclusive cover designer. That's life, but it makes it hard for us when it happens!

There are two scenarios that you may encounter. The designer is no longer available but is replying to correspondence. Or the designer is no longer available and not replying to correspondence.

If you can get the designer to reply, ask them if they can provide the source files for your past covers as a last act to you. Source files are usually Photoshop or Illustrator files, but not always. If the designer is reluctant to share the source files, offer to pay for them. Seriously.

If you can get the source files, that will make your next designer's life easier because they can match the branding with 100 percent certainty and pick up where the first designer left off without readers noticing.

If you can't get the source files, ask if they can at least provide the fonts (if you didn't get them already). You can give these to your next designer and they can use them to match branding.

If you cannot get in touch with your designer at all, you'll have to find a new designer and have a series with different branded covers on the market, which is a poor reader experience. You can either ask your new designer to match the current books as best they can, or you can have them redesign your prior titles from scratch. Either way, it's an expensive pain, but you can overcome it.

OTHER IMPORTANT COVER QUESTIONS

What if I want to design my own book cover?

I would strongly advise against designing your own cover unless you're a *book cover designer* by trade.

There's a reason you and I are authors: we're masters of the written word. Visual mediums? Probably not.

Cover design is a special skill, and unless you're willing to truly invest the time to learn how to do it on a professional level, I recommend hiring a designer.

Many authors who design their own covers usually do so for financial reasons, and that's understandable. However, if you're going to design your own covers to reduce your expenses, you have to spend more time and effort to master the learning curve. So the money you save is replaced by time and effort until you become proficient.

The last thing you want is a horrendous cover on your book. Readers equate a poor cover with poor quality, even though that may not be true.

You're a professional. Show the world your professionalism by hiring a good designer who can help you realize your artistic vision on the cover. You'll have to spend some money, but you won't rip your hair out trying to learn the nuances of Photoshop.

But if you still dare to design your own cover, read on...

What about cover templates? Can I use them to create compelling designs?

There are companies that sell cover design templates for a small fee. The templates usually come as a Microsoft Word or Adobe Photoshop file, and you can replace the template elements with your own photos, fonts, and colors. They can be helpful because you don't have to start from scratch, but you still have to do the design.

My experience is that these cover templates vary in quality. Some are poor and some are excellent.

The problem with templates is that they're not designed for your book, so you have to do a lot of work to make them look less "template-y." They can also be difficult to work with, particularly in Microsoft Word.

It's also worth noting that there are websites that allow you to design your own cover. Canva and Book Brush are two of the most prominent. These websites may also offer templates that you can use as a starting point for your cover design. They also offer a number of design tools, but are generally not as robust as a dedicated design app such as Photoshop.

Cover templates can provide a viable path to a basic book cover, but the professionalism may be questionable.

I want to use a special font on my cover, but I've heard that fonts are copyrighted. Really?

Yes, really. Some fonts, like many that are pre-installed on your computer, are in the public domain.

But font and typography creation is a little-known cottage industry, and there are designers who make money creating new fonts and licensing them.

The good news is that most book cover designers will use public domain fonts to avoid licensing expenses. There are plenty of bestselling books that have free fonts on their cover and you would never know it because the designers use effects to make them look unique.

At a minimum, it is helpful to know which fonts your designer uses on your cover so you can double-check if a license is required.

If you're designing your own cover, however, you'll want to make certain that you have a license to use the fonts on your cover. Many font sites such as Da Font provide commercial fonts for free, but there's a catch—in the fine print, it's your responsibility to pay for any licenses you may need.

. . .

If I design my own cover, how do I come up with design ideas?

Look at other covers in your genre. Then pick a few and see if you can reverse engineer some of the effects on the cover. If you're going to design your own cover, you'll have to master your design app. Learning how to imitate other designers' techniques would be my most important goal. I would recommend investing in a few design courses to give yourself a working technique set. I would also follow design blogs to stay aware of new trends.

Develop your curiosity. It will be your most important asset.

Another great resource is ALLi Design Advisor Joel Friedlander's e-book cover design awards. It's a monthly contest on his website where he judges self-published covers. He critiques bad covers too, and you can learn from his comments.

Do I need a different book cover for different countries?

Every country has its own standards on what readers prefer on book covers. For example, as a general statement, United States readers are more comfortable with guns and violent elements on book covers. Readers in other countries may not tolerate these themes.

However, my opinion is that you should avoid doing different covers for different countries.

Philosophically, it makes sense, but consider this:

• It's expensive.

• Where do you stop?

• What proof exists that your current book cover won't sell in another country? What proof exists that another cover *will*?

• You have to manage multiple editions of your book on every retailer you publish through, which is an administrative nightmare.

• How will you figure out what readers in another country want? It's an expensive mistake if you get it wrong.

As compelling as the idea might be, I don't believe it's practical for most self-published writers.

When writers license rights for foreign markets, as in traditional publishing, publishers in different countries or languages tend to use different cover editions. If you find yourself in that kind of situation, then having different covers may make sense, as you'll have a partner who has a deep understanding of foreign markets.

Must everything on my cover be visible as a thumbnail and/or in black and white?

Not really.

There are two theories here. The first is that if readers can see all the elements on your cover's thumbnail format, then your book will sell better because the thumbnail version on a book retailer search page is likely the first time readers will see your book cover.

While I *do* think having a cover optimized for thumbnails is helpful, you don't need to make all the elements readable in thumbnail format. If you do that, you risk damaging the integrity of the design.

The second theory is that your book cover should look good in grayscale because that's how e-ink devices will render it.

Have you bought an e-ink device lately? More people are reading on phones and tablets, which have color displays. In my opinion, this theory was probably true in the early days of the physical e-reader, but it's obsolete now. I still hear people say it occasionally, though, which is why I mentioned it.

What are the cover requirements for an audiobook?

Audiobook covers are perfect squares. On Audible, they should be no smaller than 2400 x 2400 pixels. On Findaway Voices, they should be no smaller than 3000 x 3000 pixels. Your safest bet would be to upload a cover that is at least 3000 x 3000 pixels, so that both Audible and Findaway Voices will accept the same file. Other audiobook retailers have similar requirements.

When should I rebrand my cover?

This is a personal question you'll have to answer depending on your circumstances.

Generally, the common advice is to change your covers every four to five years, though the mileage on certain covers will vary. You can also change them if your sales drop well below their normal level for an extended period—that may indicate that it's time for a refresh.

Rebranding a cover doesn't guarantee your sales will increase.

If you decide to rebrand, make sure you study your genre to see how it changed since you published your last book. I also recommend split-testing your new cover. If the old one still converts better, you may want to keep it until sales taper off.

In any case, rebranding is a great way to keep your books looking fresh.

When should I create the print book cover?

As tempting as it is to finish the print cover and see a proof of your print book, I recommend waiting to create your print book cover until the book is ready for publication.

Print on-demand services such as KDP Print and IngramSpark have strict formatting requirements for print books. Unlike e-book changes, which go live after a few hours, print book submissions typically require approval, which can take several days. Any time you need to make a change, you'll have to re-upload your book to get it approved.

The area where authors typically run into trouble is the page length. Print on-demand services only grant a small margin for error, so it's in your best interest to get it right the first time.

For example, let's say that you finish your book and have your designer create a print cover for a 150-page book, and you realize that your final book will be 135 pages, maybe because of editing or because you accidentally included a chapter twice.

You'll have to have your designer retool the print cover to match the new page length, and you'll have to resubmit the book for approval at KDP Print and IngramSpark. You'll incur out-of-pocket costs if your designer charges revisions, as well as revision fees at IngramSpark (if you're not an ALLi member).

While I used the example of page length, the same is also true with trim size. Make certain that the print specifications you've chosen will not change when you send the request to your designer. If not, it may cost you valuable time, money, and effort.

BOOK FORMATTING AND TYPESETTING

Formatting is important. As the last step in the publishing process before uploading your book, it's your chance to ensure that you have a great product.

The two essential elements of a properly formatted book are the same in e-book and paperback form: utility and ease of navigation.

Readers want to read a book without formatting getting in the way. They also need a good table of contents to help them navigate the book as needed.

That's it.

How do we obtain utility and ease of navigation? The answer depends on the format.

E-books are reflowable, which means that the text conforms to whatever device it is displayed on. Readers can also change the text size, font, and sizing between paragraphs.

Anything that artificially stops an e-book's reflowability is an enemy. Tabs are a prime example—they cause all sorts of problems in an e-book. The goal with an e-book is to format the text so that it appears well on any device. An e-book that reads well has utility for the reader.

Ease of navigation with e-books is all about the table of contents. An e-book usually has two types: a table of contents page that contains links to each chapter, and an NCX, which stands for navigational control XML, which allows the reader to jump between chapters on the fly no matter where they are in the book.

That's as far as I can go into this topic without boring or frustrating you—learning the art of formatting is best taught visually.

For a print book, utility comes in other forms. For example, an appropriate font, a proper font size (often 11 points), and a trim size that's comfortable to hold comprise a print book's utility. Features such as indexes, glossaries, maps, and other front and back matter elements improve a reader's enjoyment of the book.

For print book navigation, a table of contents is important (more so for nonfiction), but so are page numbers and headers so readers know where they are at all times.

In my humble opinion, whether you are reading an e-book or a print book, the best formatting is invisible and doesn't draw attention to itself.

FORMATTING E-BOOKS

Should I create my book as an EPUB, MOBI, or PDF?

The answer, as with many things in self-publishing, is all of the above.

EPUB files are the industry-standard e-book format that all retailers use, and that retailers outside of Amazon require. EPUB stands for "electronic publication."

MOBI files are Amazon's proprietary e-book format. MOBI stands for Mobipocket, which was the name of the company that originally created the format. Amazon acquired Mobipocket but didn't change the file name.

At their core, EPUBs and MOBIs are glorified HTML files that e-readers and e-reader apps render into text on the screen.

Last but not least, we have portable digital files (PDFs). PDFs were created by Adobe as a way to have a "what you see is what you get on every device" experience. No matter how or where you view a PDF, it will always look exactly the same, which is the format's major virtue.

That same virtue can make reading a PDF e-book a painful experience, but some readers prefer the format. Most apps can export PDFs with little effort, so it's a good idea to create a PDF version of your book, especially if you sell direct on your site.

Additionally, print book files must be uploaded as PDF files, and they have their own separate formatting requirements.

What tools do I need to format my book?

For an e-book, you need a word processor that can export to an e-book format. Or you need a formatting app.

Many word processors can export to EPUB. Scrivener, Ulysses, and Apple's Pages are just a few. You can use them to create a publish-ready e-book.

Microsoft Word doesn't export to EPUB unless you have a special plugin that can do it, but some retail sites such as Smashwords accept Word docs.

Word can export to HTML, however, and there are free apps like Calibre that can convert from HTML to EPUB and MOBI.

Once you have an e-book file, you can use free software like Adobe Digital Editions to see what your e-book looks like and whether you need to make changes. Amazon has a free tool called the Kindle Previewer that allows you to check MOBI files.

If you prefer to use a dedicated formatting app, you can do no better than Vellum if you have a Mac. It's the go-to app for writers to create beautiful e-books and print books. Jutoh is another alternative that is available for Mac, Windows, and Linux—but it can't do print books.

You *can* format print books in Microsoft Word, but it's not easy. A more powerful (but expensive) option for all book formatting is Adobe InDesign. Affinity Publisher is a cheaper alternative to InDesign.

What's the best way to include images in my book?

Very carefully, if you do it at all. Images are a formatter's worst nightmare. It's difficult to make them look good on all devices.

However, images may be an important part of your book, such as specialized chapter heads, illustrations, or screenshots.

Check the Resources section for a helpful article that walks you through the process of optimizing images for e-books and print.

Do I need a table of contents?

It depends on the book. Remember that for e-books there are usually two types: a table of contents page and the NCX.

For fiction, you can skip the table of contents page unless you have a special reason to include it. My opinion is that this isn't terribly useful in a fiction e-book (or print book). However, an NCX is a must-have so readers can jump between chapters if they need to.

For nonfiction, a table of contents page is essential because it gives prospective readers a glimpse into the value your book will provide (assuming your chapters are titled appropriately). An NCX is also a must for e-books.

Where should I place my table of contents in the e-book edition? At the front of the book or the back?

Which team of writers are you on? Team Front or Team Back?

This topic has been hotly debated since I became a writer, and both sides are adamant.

Team Front says that you should include the table of contents page at the front of your book because it's traditional and readers expect it.

Team Back says that you should put your table of contents page at the back of the book so readers can experience more pages of your book when they download a sample or use Amazon's Look Inside feature.

I've never seen any conclusive evidence to support either side, so I'll let you choose. I'm on Team Front, especially for nonfiction.

However, I will point out that almost everyone agrees that this debate is for e-books only. I would *not* put your table of contents at the back of your print book—it won't do readers any good!

In what order should I arrange my front and back matter?

There is an industry-standard order for your front and back matter elements. In his excellent book *The Book Blueprint: Expert Advice for Creating Industry-Standard Print Books*, ALLi Design Advisor Joel Friedlander lays out the correct order for front and back matter.

For front matter, the correct order is: half title, frontispiece (small illustration that faces the title pages), title page, copyright page, dedication, epigraph, table of contents, list of figures, list of tables, foreword, preface, acknowledgments, introduction, prologue, second half title, and finally the book itself.

Whew! I don't know about you, but that list makes me tired!

For back matter, the order is: epilogue, afterword, conclusion, postscript, appendix or addendum, chronology, notes, glossary, bibliography, list of contributors, index, errata, and colophon.

Are your eyes hurting yet?

You don't have to include all of the front or back matter elements in your book, and you probably shouldn't. Just know that this is the order that your included elements should appear in.

There are authors who choose to put some of the traditional front matter at the back of the book to maximize the e-book sample. This is especially relevant for short books.

I recommend you check out Joel's book to learn more about each of the elements. While his orders are for print books, I still think it's prudent to follow them for e-books as well.

Check the Resources section for three great resources to help you memorize and master the front and back matter elements!

Do I need different editions of my e-book for different devices?

In other words, do you need a Kindle edition of your book for e-readers, a Kindle app edition for smartphones, a computer edition for desktops, and so on?

No. The beauty of e-books is that, when formatted correctly, they change their shape according to the container. You only need one EPUB edition of your e-book, and if formatted properly, it will render similarly on any device readers use.

Every retailer has different formatting requirements for Word docs, but if you're uploading an EPUB, then you can usually bypass those requirements, as retailers will sell your EPUB as is.

What's the best font for my e-book's interior?

Readers can and will change the font of their e-books to suit their preferences. That's one of the great benefits of e-books.

You need to ensure that you use a simple font that won't create issues when it is converted to the font of the reader's choice.

My go-to choices are Palatino and Baskerville because most e-readers and e-reader apps support them, so I know there won't be conversion issues.

Just remember: readers likely won't read your book in the font you intended, and that's OK!

My book's file size is really large and Amazon is deducting big delivery fees from my sales. How do I reduce my book's file size?

Amazon prefers e-books to be as small as possible. To incentivize this, they charge a "delivery fee" of (at time of writing) $0.15 US/£0.10 per megabyte. If your e-book is 1 megabyte, Amazon will subtract $0.15 or £0.10 from every sale. If your book is six megabytes, they will subtract $0.90 or £0.60 from every sale. Ouch!

One option is to choose the 35 percent royalty option so that you won't be charged delivery fees, but then you'll take home even less money.

For this reason, it's in your best interest to keep your e-book file size as small as possible.

If you find Amazon deducting big fees, here's what I would consider.

Do you have images in your book, or is it text only? If your book is text only and racking up big delivery fees, there's likely a problem with the word processor you're using. Find out how you can get the word processor to create smaller files.

If you have images in your book, do you really need them? Specialized touches such as chapter headings and section break images are nice, but they're not essential. Cut any image that does not serve your content.

For images that do serve your content, have they been compressed and optimized for e-books? For example, one of the most common images authors use is the book cover for their next book in their back matter. It adds a nice touch and it's a smart marketing move. However, if you use the high resolution JPEG file your designer provided you, then you're not using a compressed image, and it will cost you dearly in delivery fees. Check the Resources section for a helpful resource on optimizing your images for e-book format.

Reducing your file size isn't hard. You just have to learn how to do it. Doing this will save you a *lot* of money over the years.

Should I hire a formatter or typesetter?

It depends on your skill level in formatting your book.

Most apps make it easy to create an e-book. Print books are more complicated.

A formatter or typesetter can help you create a professional-looking book, as well as add some flair that formatting apps can't do. Some genres such as poetry and illustrated children's books can be difficult to format, and it might make sense to hire a formatter.

Formatters are usually affordable. The cost varies, depending on the length of your book and any complexities, such as images.

Hiring a formatter has one major drawback, though—if you need to make a change to your book, your formatter has to do it, and they may charge you. Some formatters will allow you a certain number of revisions before charging a fee.

Even with good editing, a book can still have errors that aren't discovered until after publication. Is it worth it to you to pay a formatter for minor typo changes, not to mention the inconvenience? Also, formatters will typically not provide access to your source files, so you have to remember that too, in case they go out of business. Long term, you may lose access to your files. Negotiate at the start to receive the source files on completion, so that, if you need to, you can hire another formatter to make changes in future.

If you decide to hire a formatter, be sure to check ALLi's Service Ratings Directory.

. . .

Does ALLi recommend using templates for formatting or typesetting?

There are companies and designers who create book formatting templates, usually as a Microsoft Word file, to ease the burden of formatting. The hard, highly technical work is done for you. All you have to do is insert your manuscript, make some minor changes, and you have a publish-ready book.

Formatting templates exist for e-books and print books. My experience is that they range from poor to good. The key is picking one that looks good and is easy to manipulate. I used print book templates early in my writing journey, and while they didn't look amazing, they did look respectable. The templates were affordable and I'm glad I used them because the end product looked better than anything I could have done on my own from scratch.

It's worth noting that good formatting and typesetting software like Vellum renders templates unnecessary.

TYPESETTING PRINT BOOKS

What's the best font for my print book's interior?

Unlike e-books, where readers can change the font to suit their preferences, print book formatting is fixed.

There are two types of fonts: serif and sans serif. It's helpful to explain this before answering the question.

Serifs are ornaments that appear on certain letters. Pick any novel off your bookshelf and pay very close attention to the letters. Then go to any major website and look at the letters there.

The letters in the book you reviewed will almost always have embellishments, and slight strokes that seem to dig into the page, like on "g"s and "t"s. Those embellishments are serifs, which indicates a serif font. Look at the "g"s and "t"s on the website you chose and you will likely not see those embellishments. That means you're looking at a sans serif font.

Serif fonts are customary for printed books because they originate from handwriting and the early days of typesetting. They just look better on the printed page. Baskerville and Garamond are iconic serif fonts, and very safe choices to use in your paperback.

Sans serif fonts are better for digital reading and easier on the eyes because they are blockier. Arial and Helvetica are iconic sans serif fonts. Using a serif font on, say, a website or blog isn't completely forbidden, but it would have to be the right font or it might be difficult to read.

So: why does an author need to know about this, or even care?

First, I would make sure that you use serif fonts in your print book text. It's the industry standard. Generally speaking, sans serif fonts for the main text in print books make you look amateurish.

Second—as a side note, depending on your genre, your book cover will have serif or sans serif fonts too. Knowing whether your genre usually has a serif or sans serif font is useful to know when you are providing instructions to your cover designer.

To put a final cap on this question, use a serif font such as Baskerville or Garamond in your print book's interior. You can never go wrong with either of them, and readers won't question them. Research classic serif fonts and use the one you feel most comfortable with.

Skip fonts like Times New Roman, Arial, or Helvetica because they'll make even the most distinguished book look like a high school essay.

What's the most common print book trim size for a self-published book?

The trim size is the physical measurement of your book.

The most common choice is 6 x 9 inches , but there are other common sizes such as 5.25 x 8 and 5 x 8. Look at the paperbacks in your genre to see the sizes that readers are buying.

Should I create a large-print edition of my book?

To make sure I'm extra clear with this answer, large-print editions are print books. For e-books, readers can change the font size as they see fit.

Large-print editions are popular with readers who struggle to read smaller print. It's an underserved market.

Typically, the font size is 16 points or higher and the trim size is bigger.

Whether you should create a large-print edition is entirely based on your genre and your target audience, as you will have to incur additional expense to create it. If your readers ask you for it, that's another indicator that it might be a good idea.

I've included an article in the Resources section by ALLi's Author Enterprise Advisor Joanna Penn about her experience publishing large-print editions of her fiction. I've also included a great article by one of our ALLi members about publishing dyslexia-friendly books, which is a similar issue that you might want to consider depending on your genre and target audience needs.

How can I create a hardcover edition of my book?

Readers love hardcover editions. They're sturdier, have collection value, and they look great on a bookshelf.

Hardcover editions have different requirements from paperbacks, though, particularly with the book cover. Hardcovers can be case-wrapped, meaning the cover design is printed directly on the front and back cover of the book, or they can have dust-jackets, which are removable sleeves that contain the cover design. There are other unique variations and features that are unique to hardcovers.

Generally speaking, the trim sizes can be the same as paperbacks. You may have to create a separate formatting file for your hardcover, but the process is the same as a paperback.

If you want to create a hardcover edition, I recommend hiring a cover designer to help you, especially if you want a dust jacket.

At the time of this writing, Amazon KDP Print does not offer a hardcover option. ALLi's recommendation is to use IngramSpark. They're a phenomenal distributor and allows you to create hardcovers. However, as with all titles published on IngramSpark, you have to pay setup and revision fees every time you need to make a change. This can add up, so it pays to make sure your files are right the first time.

Fun fact: IngramSpark waives setup and revision fees for ALLi members. If you publish just a few paperbacks or hardcovers per year, this benefit alone will pay for the cost of ALLi membership. Just sayin'.

What are some rookie mistakes indie writers make when formatting or typesetting their books?

This is not an exhaustive list, but here are some mistakes that will make your book look amateurish.

For e-books:

• Double-spaced line sizing.

• Including page numbers. E-books don't have "pages" because they're reflowable.

• No table of contents page (especially for nonfiction).

• No NCX.

• Tabs (this creates formatting problems).

• No page breaks between chapters.

• Images that are too small or too large.

• Broken or outdated hyperlinks. Always triple-check your links!

• Long and ugly links. Use a simple link, a link shortener, or, if you must, embed the link within the text itself.

• A call to action that says your next book is "Coming soon"… when it's already published. Avoid referencing future dates in your book, especially because readers may buy your book today but not read it for many months or years into the future, and you have no way of guaranteeing that they will be reading the most up-to-date version, even if you update it.

For print books:

• Inappropriate line spacing.

• Inappropriate fonts, such as Times New Roman, Arial, Helvetica, or, worst of all, Comic Sans. Traditional publishers wouldn't be caught dead using these fonts in their books.

• No table of contents (for nonfiction).

• No page numbers.

• Incorrect order of front and back matter.

• Running headers and footers on the first page of a chapter (that's a big no-no).

• Deep links. Readers can't tap on links like they can with e-books. Keep your links limited to the domain name or a simple, first level page name, like ALLi's Service Ratings Directory. Also, make sure that your links aren't a different color, as it will look bad on the printed page.

• Using phrases like "click here" or "tap here." Readers can't do that in a print book. I shouldn't have to say this, but it happens more often than it should.

• Not reviewing your proofs before publishing. Take some time to review them, as it's an opportunity to catch a few typos.

• Excessive typos. Typos aren't a formatting issue per se, but they look particularly bad in print books.

There are more rookie errors, but if you can avoid all of these, your book will create a great experience for readers.

PART IV

BOOK PRODUCTION AND DISTRIBUTION

YOUR BOOK, ALL OVER THE WORLD

We are fortunate as authors today to live in the greatest era of book distribution. Excellent distribution options are available to indie authors for e-books, audiobooks, and print-on-demand. If you can dream it, you can get your self-published book distributed there with ease: Amazon, Apple, Google Play, Kobo, Overdrive, to name a few.

Publishing platforms like Kobo have relationships with book retailers in countries all over the world. Through IngramSpark it's possible to get your book into bookstores worldwide too. There are challenges to this route, certainly, and it's hard work, but it is possible.

ALLi's guiding policy for the most effective distribution plan is to be in as many formats as you can—e-book, print, and audio—and in as many stores as you can, while making your own website the core of your bookselling operation.

Those who don't want the hassle of dealing with multiple platforms individually can use a service known as an aggregator. Aggregators are companies like Draft2Digital, PublishDrive, and StreetLib that allow you to upload your book onto one single dashboard, which then automatically distributes it to hundreds of outlets all over the world.

In short, there is an abundance of distribution options for your book.

I'm confused about distributors, wholesalers, and retailers. Who does what?

Some of the platforms open to indie authors are production, distribution, and bookselling platforms. And some companies refer to themselves as publishers, when they are really printers or author services. As a result, authors can confuse the different parties involved in self-publishing.

Here's the deal:

- You, the author, are the *publisher*.
- The platforms you use for production, printing, distribution, marketing, or other aspects of the publishing process are *self-publishing services*.
- The wholesalers, distributors, and aggregators that supply books are all *distribution channels* as far as an author is concerned.
- Bookstores, including online stores, and libraries are *outlets*.
- Some self-publishing services like IngramSpark are both a publishing service and a distributor. Others like Amazon KDP, Apple Books, Google Play, and Kobo are self-publishing services and distributors with online retail store outlets attached. It is for this reason that ALLi recommends you should go directly to these companies, rather than through an aggregator. Kobo, uniquely, in addition to being service, distributor, and online retailer, also partners with other book retailers and distributors around the world, like Walmart in the United States and WHSmith in the United Kingdom.

What is the difference between a book wholesaler and a book distributor?

These services grew up in traditional publishing and are less relevant in digital self-publishing. A wholesaler works for bookstores and libraries and other book outlets. They buy books from a publisher and sell them to their customers. A distributor works for the publisher, supplying books to the market and taking a fee and a percentage for the distribution service. They may also provide other billable services.

How should I price my book?

People talk about pricing a lot and often make the assumption that pricing cheaper means more readers and more profit in the end. Not always.

Some retailers, like Amazon, attract bargain hunters, while others like Kobo and Apple are far less price sensitive. An e-book under 50,000 words priced at $2.99 might be considered too expensive on Amazon, but may do well on Apple Books or Kobo.

On those platforms, the psychology of pricing relates to quality and value. Certain readers comparing two books may go with the higher-priced option and may assume it's a better book.

There's no hard guideline for pricing your book, but there are some universal rules of thumb.

For e-books, the general sweet spot for indie books is between $2.99 and $9.99. Most books fall between $2.99 and $5.99, with box sets and omnibuses priced more toward $9.99. The best way to find your pricing sweet spot is to see how other, well-selling *self-published* books in your genre are priced. That's direct evidence of what readers are willing to pay.

Why is $2.99 to $9.99 the best price point? Unfortunately, at the time of this writing, $9.99 is the last price point where Amazon offers a 70 percent sales commission for self-published writers. For all price points under $2.99 and over $9.99, you'll only receive a 35 percent sales commission on Amazon. Some retailers such as Kobo are more generous with their sales commission above $9.99, so you should take that into consideration if you have a book that you feel may be worth more than that.

Also, many traditionally published books are priced north of $9.99, so you'll make your book more attractive by comparison if you price it slightly lower.

For e-books, I recommended pricing *lower* than traditionally published titles. For print books, that's still true, but you can and should charge more than for your e-book. Readers will pay more for print books. Higher-priced print books also make your e-book look cheaper by comparison.

For print books, you also have to think about making them attractive to booksellers, which means pricing them high enough that they can make a decent profit (for you *and* the bookseller). This generally means somewhere between $10 and $20 for the book, depending on the length and printing requirements.

For audiobooks, it depends on where you publish. You cannot control your pricing on Audible audiobooks, which is unfortunate because Audible (owned by Amazon) is the largest audiobook retailer at the time of this writing. Pricing there is based on the length of your book. But if you distribute to other audiobook retailers, you can set a price.

Don't be afraid to experiment with promotional pricing on all your formats. Sometimes breaking the rules can work. Be flexible and be open to trying different things.

What matters most is what readers think is acceptable and reasonable. They'll pay $2.99 to $9.99 as long as your book matches the market.

Of course, don't be silly with your pricing. Don't offer a fifty-page book for $9.99, for example. Readers will punish you in reviews, or not buy your book at all.

As a very general rule, longer books *can* be priced higher. They take more time and money to write, edit, and produce—and you should be compensated for that.

If your book is way longer than comparable books in your genre, then maybe you *can* get a dollar or more extra for it. If it's way shorter, then maybe you can charge less as a value to readers. But I wouldn't make length your *primary* consideration.

For nonfiction like self-help and business books, and for poetry, the length of the book matters less than its effect or perceived value. If your book is short, but the reader feels it could profoundly change their life, or inspire them, or enable them to make more money, they will be willing to pay a higher price.

And of course, established authors have fans who are often willing to pay more. They know what to expect and they can't wait. But don't price your book lower just because you're a beginner—you will leave money on the table.

As with most things in publishing, you need to know your genre and reader expectations to make the wisest choice for you.

A final pricing tip is to use "pretty pricing" for the major international currencies (such as pounds, euros, yen, pesos, US dollars, Canadian dollars, and Australian dollars). Don't use the automatic currency conversion that retailers offer. For example, instead of selling your book for 2.84 euros, round up to 2.99. It looks more professional and will probably convert better.

(See also "How should I price my book to sell more?" in the Book Promotion chapter)

I want to make changes to my book. Do I need a second edition?

New editions are common in fiction and nonfiction.

You may decide to refresh your nonfiction book with more up-to-date content several years after publication, or you might add, remove, or improve sections in your novel.

The general rule is that if the edits you're making would render the book substantially different, then a new edition is needed.

• • •

For second editions, should I unpublish my first edition?

If a new edition is needed, then yes, you should unpublish the first edition so that readers don't accidentally buy the wrong edition. It's also your opportunity to refresh the book by putting the new edition number on the cover and in your book description. Think of it as a new marketing opportunity.

Readers of the older edition might even be interested in falling in love with it all over again!

How do I get my book into libraries?

Libraries have strict purchasing guidelines, and they use special catalogues to buy their books. You can get your book into those catalogues—all it takes is having the knowledge. Don't visit your local library with copies of your book. In a librarian's eyes, only an amateur would do that.

Pricing your book at the right price for librarians is also another helpful tip.

Library distribution is beyond the scope of this book but ALLi has a guide called *Your Book in Libraries* which is referenced in the Resources section. I've included some other links there to help you explore this further.

Help! Someone is pirating my book!

Every writer gets pirated. It's an unfortunate consequence of publishing books in the digital age.

E-book piracy is rampant, and there isn't much we can do about it. Trying to get your books taken down from pirate sites is like the worst game of whack-a-mole ever. You'll waste a lot of money trying to sue infringers too, especially if they live in other countries.

As much as I'd like to advise you otherwise, the best course of action is usually to do nothing.

To make matters worse, just because a piracy website says your book is available doesn't mean your book is *available*. Some sites are notorious for using a book cover as bait to get someone to download the "book," only for the downloaded file to be a virus instead... with no book to be found. Unless you want to risk getting a virus yourself, you have no way of verifying that your book is actually being pirated.

Combine this with the fact that you're not battling pirates anymore— there isn't some shady person uploading your book to the cloud. These days, it's sophisticated bots and scripts. That makes the battle all the more unwinnable.

If your book is pirated, some argue that downloaders would have never bought the book in the first place, which I think is true.

If you explore that argument further, downloaders could be a completely different audience who might appreciate your work, if you accept them as they are. It's hard to really know for sure.

Getting your book pirated is a rite of passage. As I heard an ALLi member say once, it means you've finally arrived!

A publisher has republished my self-published book because I signed a deal. Should I remove the original book from the market?

So a traditional publisher has bought the rights to your already-self-published work. Great!

If the publisher holds the rights to the book, you can no longer sell it yourself on retailers. Your contract should stipulate when you need to bring it down. Earn your sales commissions until the last minute if you can, and then make sure you fulfill your contractual obligations.

What is hybrid publishing and should I consider it?

A hybrid publisher is a publisher who provides a mix of traditional and self-publishing services, usually in the same contract. It is commonly confused with the term "hybrid author," who is an author who has both traditionally and self-published books.

A hybrid publisher helps an author self-publish their book, for example, but may take a percentage of royalties in exchange for the assistance.

This is a relatively new field that is fraught with contractual dangers, so always use ALLi's Self-Publishing Service Ratings Directory when deciding on whether a hybrid publishing service is legitimate or not.

Amazon won't remove my old book, even though it's now listed as "unavailable." What can I do?

There's nothing you can do, unfortunately. Amazon prides itself on being the biggest bookstore on Earth. That means cataloguing and carrying every book in existence, whether it's in print or not.

Amazon will not remove older editions of books for one simple reason: someone might have a used copy to sell. Removing the title from sale deprives someone somewhere in the world of that opportunity.

Many authors have "unavailable" books. It's a rite of passage. My best advice is to focus on writing more books.

Help! Amazon is threatening to shut down my account!

Amazon may occasionally take action on accounts that it feels are violating its terms of service. Sometimes this is driven by Amazon employees; sometimes it's driven by an algorithm.

Assuming that you have *not* violated the KDP terms of service, contact Amazon to get more information about why your account is being terminated. They may not give you very much information. Be prepared for that—Amazon generally takes a "guilty until proven innocent" mentality on account terminations, probably because it's effective for eliminating the bad actors. It's not much consolation to innocent people caught in a misunderstanding, though.

Be persistent. Use every avenue that you can, and explain your side of the matter, with as much evidence as possible that you are not guilty.

If you're an ALLi member and can't seem to reverse the termination, write to ALLi in confidence using the form on our contact page at selfpublishingadvice.org/contact. ALLi has a mediation relationship with Amazon and can help advocate on your behalf (yet another reason you should become a member!).

It goes without saying that you should always make sure you follow the KDP terms of service to the letter and don't deviate from them. Every once in a while, new and shiny marketing techniques emerge that promise to make you money but may be a violation of KDP's terms. Resist the temptation, even if everyone else is doing it. If Amazon takes action on your account one day, you won't be able to defend yourself.

Being on the verge of termination is not a position you ever want to be in. It can ruin your author business, especially if you're exclusive to Amazon.

ALL ABOUT ISBNS

ISBN-related questions are the most commonly received on our #AskALLi Member Q&A. I am going to do my best to answer the top ISBN questions here!

What is an ISBN?

ISBN stands for *International Standard Book Number*. It is a unique numeric identifier attached to a book. The purpose of the ISBN is to establish and identify one title or edition of a book from one specific publisher.

Each ISBN is unique to that edition of a book, enabling tracking and marketing of books by booksellers, libraries, universities, wholesalers, and distributors.

There are over 160 ISBN agencies worldwide, each appointed as the exclusive agent responsible for assigning ISBNs to publishers in their country or geographic territory. In some countries, like Canada and France, ISBNs are issued for free. In others, like the United Kingdom and the United States, they are issued by private companies: Nielsen and Bowker, respectively. Both charge money to issue ISBNs.

An ISBN can be purchased by the author and used on any retailer. Amazon also, like other retailers such as Ingram, Smashwords, and BookBaby, purchase ISBNs to issue to authors for their print book titles.

Amazon also runs its own book number system for e-books on its online store, called the Amazon Standard Identification Number (ASIN). The ASIN is used only on Amazon.

Do I need an ISBN?

While technically you don't need an ISBN to publish a book, ALLi recommends that you do purchase and use your own ISBNs, and that you use one ISBN for each format (hardcover, paperback, e-book, audiobook, etc). Owning your own ISBN makes you the publisher of record, rather than the self-publishing service you've used to produce, distribute, or sell your book.

One of the biggest advantages of self-publishing is that you are the publisher, retaining all rights. Why then allow somebody else to be identified as the publisher?

Owning your own ISBNs means your books can circulate properly in the industry supply chain. You can also freely work with bookstores and libraries, who use ISBNs to select the format of book they want to purchase.

In these outlets, and all book distribution ecosystems, ISBNs help with discoverability, sales, and analysis.

Not owning your own ISBNs adds to indie author invisibility. The ISBN agencies in many countries provide reports on the publishing industry each year based on ISBN tracking. Since many indie authors do not use ISBNs for their e-books, the indie world remains a "shadow industry" that is untracked on official reports. This gives rise to many misleading headlines about indie publishing and author income.

. . .

Does the ISBN protect my copyright?

No. It is an identifier and a product code only. There is no legal requirement for an ISBN and it conveys no form of legal or copyright protection. It is simply a product identification number. Copyright automatically belongs to you as the author.

(See the Copyright and Contracts chapter for more information on copyright.)

Who is eligible to purchase ISBNs?

Any individual or organization who is publishing a qualifying product for general sale or distribution (as defined by ISBN agencies) is eligible to purchase an ISBN. The publisher of the book is generally the person or organization taking the financial risk in making a publication available.

According to Nielsen, any publication that is without a defined end should not be assigned an ISBN.

According to Nielsen's website, some examples of products that do NOT qualify for ISBNs include:

- Journals, periodicals, serials, newspapers in their entirety (single issues or articles, where these are made available separately, may qualify for an ISBN).
- Abstract entities such as textual works and other abstract creations of intellectual or artistic content.
- Ephemeral printed materials such as advertising matter and the like.
- Customized print on-demand publications. (Publications that are available only on a limited basis, such as customized print on-demand publications with content specifically tailored to a user's request, shall not be assigned an ISBN.)
- Printed music.
- Art prints and art folders without title page and text.

- Personal documents (such as a curriculum vitae or personal profile).
- Greeting cards.
- Music sound recordings.
- Software that is intended for any purpose other than educational or instructional.
- Electronic bulletin boards.
- Emails and other digital correspondence.
- Updating websites.
- Games.

Do authors need an ISBN for all books?

Of course, there are exceptions. The decision to use your own ISBN, or even whether to use one at all for e-books, is a personal decision each author must make. Here are a few situations to help you decide.

- If you plan on only producing one book, in e-book format only (no print book or audio), and budgeting is a consideration, you might consider a free ISBN from a supplier like Amazon KDP or IngramSpark.
- If you just want to print a book for family, friends, or community, and don't intend to sell it online or through stores, you don't need an ISBN.
- If you are planning to be an indie author for the long term, you should purchase your own ISBNs.
- If you are concerned about long-term visibility and discoverability through SEO as well as customer, bookstore, and library searches, you should buy your own ISBNs.
- If your strategy includes aggressive marketing into brick-and-mortar stores and/or libraries, you definitely need your own ISBNs.

How much does an ISBN cost?

It varies from country to country. ISBNs in the United States are the most expensive. In some countries such as Canada and France, you can get ISBNs for free. Visit your local ISBN agency's website for more details.

Can I just use one ISBN for all the formats of my book?

No. You are required to use a different ISBN for each edition. That is one of the major functions of the ISBN. If your book is available in paperback and audio, you need a separate ISBN for each format.

Can I use the same ISBN for a translated book in the same format?

No. Again, each translation needs to be identified separately and so requires its own separate ISBN.

I'm reprinting a book but adding a new chapter—do I need a new ISBN?

Yes, if what you are adding is substantial. Whenever you add or remove a significant amount of material and alter the content of the book significantly, you need a new ISBN.

I'm republishing a book with a new cover design—should I change the ISBN?

No. A change of cover design with no changes to the content of the book does not require a new ISBN.

I'm changing my book's title. Do I need a new ISBN?

Yes. A title change qualifies as a substantial change.

. . .

I'm changing the binding on the book to paperback rather than hardback (with no other changes). Do I need a new ISBN?

Yes. Changes in binding always require new ISBNs.

I want to change the trim size of my paperback. Will I need a new ISBN?

Yes. Changes to trim size always require new ISBNs.

I'm changing the price—do I need a new ISBN?

No. Price changes with no other changes do not require new ISBNs.

I'm moving to another country. Can I take my ISBNs with me?

Once a book is published, there is no need to reissue its ISBN because you've moved locations. You *will* need to buy or obtain ISBNs from your new country's ISBN agency for future books that you publish, however.

I am publishing a book with another author—whose ISBN should we use?

For co-written books, both authors are allowed to each have an ISBN on the book. Or you can list just one. If you use more than one, it should be made clear which number identifies which author or publisher.

According to the International ISBN Agency, if only one author will hold physical stock and distribute the book, it is recommended that only that author's ISBN should appear on the book.

. . .

What do I do if I reprint a book with a new publishing name?

The new publisher should be listed on the title page with the relevant ISBN, but industry best practice is to also list the previous edition's publisher, ISBN, and publication date.

Industry best practices also say that a separate ISBN may be assigned if the same publication is published under a different imprint name by the same publisher, or when a publication is republished under the imprint of a different publisher.

Can I buy an ISBN on behalf of someone else?

No. An ISBN makes you the publisher of record. Once an ISBN has been issued it can't be resold, reassigned, or transferred. An imprint can be assigned, but the original ISBN owner will be listed as the publisher of record.

Do I need an ISBN to distribute to libraries?

Libraries are great outlets for indie authors. OverDrive, the biggest supplier to libraries in the world, requires an ISBN. If you choose not to use an ISBN for your e-books, you're cutting out a major distribution channel that also supplies books to retailers around the globe, including Books-A-Million, Ciando, and others. Indie authors can get into OverDrive through Kobo and other distributors and aggregators.

E-BOOK DISTRIBUTION

Should I put my books in Kindle Unlimited?

This is one of the most important early decisions you will have to make in your author business.

Do you keep your book exclusive to Amazon's KDP Select Program in exchange for the multitude of benefits and visibility the program provides, or do you "go wide" and publish your book everywhere?

For fear of making this book outdated, I won't go into the details of what KDP Select offers, as the offerings change from time to time. However, at the time of this writing, Kindle Unlimited is one of KDP Select's biggest selling points. Authors are paid based on the number of pages in their books that readers read each month. Kindle Unlimited can be lucrative, and many writers make a living on their KU income alone.

ALLi's opinion (which aligns closely with mine) is to avoid exclusivity whenever possible. Yes, it's true that KDP Select goes in ninety-day terms, so it's not permanent exclusivity, and yes, it's true that you can pull your books in and out at any time, but the best way to have a sustainable author business is to develop income from many different sources. That way, you'll be insulated somewhat if one of them dries up. If you rely on Amazon for your income, and Amazon makes a change to KDP Select, you've just lost all your income.

That said, there's nothing wrong with using KDP Select strategically. If it's your first book and you need some income to help you get on your feet, there's nothing wrong with being exclusive for a short time. But in the bigger picture of your career, you'll do yourself more favors long term by being nonexclusive and diversifying your income.

A common counterargument to this is that, if you go wide, you don't make money at other retailers that matches what you can make on Amazon. While that may be true in the short term, it's also true that it takes a long time to build an audience on other retailers, sometimes many years. The longer you wait to go wide, the longer it will take you to build those audiences.

If I put my book in KDP Select, can I publish it anywhere else?

No and yes.

You cannot publish your *e-book* anywhere else if you are enrolled in KDP Select. There is no way around this, and if you try to circumvent it, you will get a nasty letter from Amazon. They might even terminate your account.

However, Amazon exclusivity is for your e-book only. That means you can still publish your paperback, hardcover, and audiobook anywhere you like.

How can I make my e-book free?

Free books can be a good promotional tool. Some authors like to make a certain book in their catalogue permanently free ("permafree") to drive sales for their other books.

Many retailers allow you to set your book's price to free.

Amazon, however, does not, but its bots will price-match your book if it is offered for lower somewhere else. If you set your book for free on other retailers, Amazon will eventually price-match your book.

Should I use an e-book aggregator or go direct to book retailers like Apple Books and Google Play?

e-book distributors (also known as e-book aggregators) are a great way to expand your reach. Sites like PublishDrive, Draft2Digital, and StreetLib allow you to upload your book once, and they distribute it to many of the major retailers in exchange for a commission. They can get your book into retailers that you can't on your own, ones you've probably never even heard of.

All e-book aggregators have unique offerings and you need to investigate which one is best for you.

To answer the question of whether to use an aggregator or go direct, why not both? Wherever possible, I recommend uploading directly to a retailer if they offer a dashboard. You'll have more control. Use the e-book aggregators to expand your reach into markets you can't tap directly.

Google Play keeps discounting my e-book. What do I do?

Google Play uses a different pricing model than other retailers. It's called the wholesale model, which is where the book publisher sets a recommended price of the book, but the retailer can discount the price in order to sell it.

On Amazon (for e-books), you set the price of your book, and Amazon takes a commission. This is how most retailers operate and it's called agency pricing. Amazon doesn't discount your e-book unless your book is cheaper elsewhere. And if it is cheaper elsewhere, Amazon simply matches the price.

Google, however, uses wholesale pricing for e-books. Therefore, it will discount your book, usually to odd price points. The best way to make sure your book sells at a price point you want is to raise the price.

AUDIOBOOK DISTRIBUTION

Should I produce an audiobook, and how?

The audiobook market is experiencing exponential growth. With more people discovering the joys of listening to audio on the go, it's no surprise that authors are rushing to get their books into audio.

Many authors have been reporting growing audio sales in the past few years. Some writers can live off their audiobook sales alone.

Should you get *your* book into audio?

The answer is yes, if you can afford it.

I recommend only pursuing audio if you're willing to pay production costs out-of-pocket, which is expensive.

Royalty shares are certainly an option, but the more experienced narrators charge per finished hour (the number of hours the final audiobook will be). You can expect good narrators to start at around $200 per finished hour, and they will not accept royalty shares. With royalty shares on Audible's ACX, you lock yourself into a long exclusivity agreement. (ACX stands for Audible Creation Exchange.)

The key is to create a good audiobook product. A good narrator will help you do that.

A unique differentiator with audio is that listeners often follow narrators, and narrators often bring their own fans to each new release. This is why paying for a good narrator is important.

If you decide to do it, understand that audio isn't a magic bullet. You won't automatically get rich by putting your book into audio. As with anything you sell, your success depends on the quality and timing of your book, the marketing, and a little bit of luck.

Can I narrate an audiobook by myself?

You can, but I would advise against it unless you know what you're doing or are willing to learn.

If you write fiction, then I *especially* advise against narrating your own audiobooks unless you have the voice for it, can do many different voices, and are willing to learn audio engineering and how to create high-quality audio.

Audiobook recording isn't as simple as turning on a microphone and talking. It's highly technical and requires a certain personality type. I find that most fiction authors have no business behind a microphone reading their stories. We're *writers*, not narrators.

For nonfiction, depending on what you write, narrating your own books could be a nice selling point. But you still have to take the time to learn how to produce audiobook-quality audio.

Check the Resources section for some helpful links on getting started with narrating your own audiobooks.

How long does it take to narrate a book?

Audible uses 9,300 words per hour as the estimate for professional narrators. A 70,000-word novel will be approximately 7.5 finished hours as an audiobook. Budget about two to three times the length of the finished audiobook for total recording time to account for retakes and breaks during the session.

How do I hire a narrator?

The process for hiring usually goes like this:

- You create an account at one of the audiobook publishers or production companies.
- You find a narrator (sometimes called producer) by listening to their auditions.
- You and the narrator reach an agreement on how much they will get paid for each finished hour of the audiobook.
- The narrator records and uploads the audiobook, which you then approve. You pay the producer and receive your audio files.

How much does professional narration cost?

The cost to produce a professionally narrated audiobook depends on the length of your book, the service you use, and the quality of the narrator. Many ACX narrators are unionized and will not accept less than $250 per finished hour for audiobook projects.

Where should I distribute my audiobook?

Amazon has the lion's share of the audiobook market through Audible, but that is changing. Audiobooks.com and iTunes have the next highest shares, with services like Google Play, Kobo, Overdrive, and Scribd growing.

Your first decision will be whether you want to be exclusive to Amazon, Audible, and iTunes by distributing through ACX or whether you want to have nonexclusive distribution that will enable you to get your book on these and other retailers and services like Google Play, Kobo, Nook, Overdrive, and Scribd.

Just like e-books, the benefit to being exclusive to Amazon is that you will receive higher royalty rates. The benefit to nonexclusive distribution is that your book will be available at many more retailers.

Again, ALLi recommends nonexclusivity as the best long-term, business-building option.

Audiobook distributors like Author's Republic, Findaway Voices, ListenUp, and Kobo Writing Life are good aggregator distributors for audiobooks.

How should I price my audiobook?

On Audible, audiobooks are automatically priced according to their length. The author has no control over the price point.

Outside of the Audible ecosystem, you can price your books at whatever price point you want. Look at the other books in your genre to see what they're priced at (assuming they're not exclusive to Audible, that is).

PRINT BOOK DISTRIBUTION

How do I get my print book into bookstores?

This is such a great question that we have an entire ALLi guidebook by Debbie Young dedicated to it! It's called *Winning Shelf Space: Get Your Self-Published Book into Book Stores*. Check the Resources section for a link to buy (ALLi members get this book, and all ALLi guidebooks, free).

In summary, to get your book into bookstores, you'll need to use IngramSpark, price your book in such a way that booksellers receive an attractive discount so they can make a profit, and ensure your book is as professional-looking as possible. That's just the surface, though, and Debbie will walk you through the details.

For the love of all that is holy in the world, do not visit a bookstore to convince them to buy your books. Please. That brands you as an amateur and it will ensure that the bookseller will not stock your books. There's a more professional, industry-standard way of doing it. Read Debbie's book to find out how.

. . .

How do I make it easy for a bookstore to carry my book without bearing the financial burden of returns?

The returns system is costly. Bookstores generally won't purchase a book unless it can be returned. If a book doesn't sell, bookstores can't sell the unsold copies, so they return them to the publisher at the publisher's expense. (Read: you!)

At this point, a traditional publisher has lost their ability to make a profit, so they must do whatever they can to recoup some costs by "remaindering" the books, which means selling them at a steeply discounted cost. Authors don't have that luxury.

Often, remaindered books are destroyed.

This system can completely devastate an indie author, so it is best to avoid it unless you know what you're doing. For this reason, I recommend you do NOT allow returns unless you are specifically targeting physical bookstores for your sales, and have a business plan that takes account of returns. You cannot do this with print-on-demand books.

KDP Print vs IngramSpark: Which is better for paperback distribution?

KDP Print is Amazon's book distribution arm and it ensures delivery to Amazon customers in many countries, through their online retail stores, in return for a commission on each book sold. IngramSpark has the world's largest distribution network of paperback books. It distributes to bookstores, and can also distribute to Amazon and other online retailers.

The downside to IngramSpark is that it does not have an owned sales platform like Amazon. Also, its platform is less user friendly and it charges setup fees and revision fees for each book (though not to ALLi members, for whom all fees are waived).

ALLi does recommend distributing through IngramSpark because of its global distribution network. In fact, Amazon is one of Ingram's biggest customers, using Ingram publishing services to produce paperbacks for the KDP Print expanded distribution service, and many Amazon imprints.

Both Ingram and Amazon offer multiple standard and nonstandard trim sizes, and both offer glossy and matte cover options. I find the difference in print quality to be negligible. Both platforms provide good customer service should a batch of books prove defective— always a possibility with any print order.

IngramSpark offers some extras: hardcover books (clothbound with a dustcover or casebound where the cover image is printed on the hardcover) and large-print books, which are popular with libraries.

Both platforms require the same elements to set up a book (interior file, cover file, metadata) but KDP Print makes the publishing process far easier.

ALLi recommends using both IngramSpark and Amazon KDP together to maximize exposure for your books.

Some bookstores refuse to stock books distributed by KDP Print because of a bias against Amazon. If your book is available through IngramSpark, you won't have this problem. Bookstores may still have a bias against self-published books, but you can at least clear the first hurdle of getting in their catalogue, so if a reader asks for your book, the store can order it.

How do I use both KDP Print and IngramSpark together?

To use KDP for Amazon sales only, when setting up your book in KDP Print, do NOT enable KDP's "expanded distribution." Expanded distribution is actually provided to KDP Print by IngramSpark. As a self-publishing author, you have the option to go direct to IngramSpark instead.

Then, when setting up your book on IngramSpark, opt in to all other sales channels *except* Amazon.

PART V

BOOK MARKETING AND PROMOTION

BOOK MARKETING

Before we delve into the marketing and promotion questions, we need to define our terms. People use these terms loosely and often mix them up.

Marketing and promotion are separate stages in ALLi's seven stages of publishing. Each has a distinct function, as explained in Orna's book *Creative Self-Publishing*.

Book marketing is ongoing, repeatable activity that generates awareness of a book and its author among book distributors, retailers, and readers. Marketing positions you as an author, and your books as what the publishing business calls "discoverable"—which means they can be easily found by readers who are searching for a book like yours. Marketing covers ongoing activity like tending to your website, your regular social media activity, and growing and communicating with your email list.

Book promotion is concentrated sales-driven activity behind a particular book for a particular period of time. Promotion takes one book and brings it to its target readers, with enticement to buy.

It covers things like advertising, price promotions, a BookBub deal, blog tours, or real-life book tours.

— ORNA ROSS, *CREATIVE SELF-PUBLISHING*

You can promote your book to everyone in the world, but if you don't do the essential work of the marketing process, all your promotions will fall short.

This is why ALLi treats marketing and promotion as two separate and distinct phases of the publishing process.

How do you balance writing and marketing?

When you're writing your first book, the natural tendency is to put all of your energy into writing and getting the book ready for publication. That's normal.

When you publish your book, however, now you have some difficult questions to answer: do you start writing the next book or do you market your first book? How much time should you spend marketing versus writing?

These are deceptively difficult questions, actually, especially if you are a part-time writer and have limited time to write.

I've seen some writers divide their time 50–50, 60–40, or 70–30 between writing and marketing. I've also seen writers schedule specific time on their calendar for marketing.

The most common advice, however, and the most practical in my opinion, is to structure your marketing so that you can do one thing per day that will help you sell more books.

For example, you might send an email to ten book bloggers every day until there are no more to email. This might take you 15 to 20 minutes a day. Or, you might spend 10 minutes per day tweaking your Amazon ads. The key is to keep it simple.

Marketing doesn't have to be overwhelming. Breaking it into small chunks is a smart strategy. Just like you can exercise with 15 minutes a day, or learn to write your book in 15-minute increments, so too can you market with small amounts of time.

When is the best time to start marketing my book?

Now. Right now.

It's never too early to start marketing your book. That's right, I'm telling you to start marketing your book even if you're not finished with your first draft!

There's a principle in marketing called the Rule of Seven. It means that customers need to see your product seven times on average before buying. The Rule of Seven applies specifically to advertising, but generally speaking, it's good practice to start talking about your book early and often so that readers will have repeated exposure to it by the time you publish.

Inevitably, the next questions are: "What if I'm an unknown?" "What if I don't have a platform?" "Why should anyone listen to me?"

It's OK to start marketing when you're an unknown. It's not a waste of time. In fact, if no one is watching, it allows you to make some critical mistakes and learn from them.

If you don't have a platform, that's OK too, because now's the time to build it, which leads us to the next question…

What is an author platform and how can I build one?

Your author platform is your home base. It's where readers can go first to learn anything and everything about you.

A platform consists of several components:

- Your website.

- Your mailing list or online community.
- A tribe-building medium such as a blog, podcast, or YouTube channel.
- Social media channels.

Out of those elements, only a *website* is required. Contrary to what others tell you, you don't have to do anything you don't want to do. Building your author platform is a Choose Your Own Adventure of sorts. No author's platform will (or should) look the same.

Your website is required because it's where you can showcase your books. It tells readers who you are, where to find your books, what's new with you, and how to contact you. If you want to be taken seriously as a writer, you need a website.

Years ago, it used to be fairly common for writers *not* to have websites. Today, it's far less common.

A *mailing list* is still pretty important these days. Email isn't dead. In fact, it's the only way to get in touch with some people. A mailing list allows you to email your biggest fans every time you have a new release. If you're a newbie, you might not have very many people on your list at first, but as your journey progresses, your list can grow over time and can make you a lot of money.

Think about it like this: a reader finishes your book and LOVES it. Shouldn't they have a way to find out when you have a new release? Exactly! Mailing lists are for the most devoted fans. We'll talk about them in more depth later in this chapter.

A *tribe-building medium* is how you start building influence as a writer. A blog, podcast, or YouTube channel is a great way to communicate actively with your readers. It's also another channel to contact people who may not check their emails often. Many writers use Facebook communities as well, and these communities are great ways to build engagement around your books.

Lastly, we have *social media channels*. We'll cover social media later, but for now, just know that it's yet another channel to reach people, especially if you use multiple networks. I personally don't recommend using social media as your sole way of building a platform because you can lose your entire audience overnight if one of the networks makes a major change. Plus, you don't own your audience on places like Facebook or Instagram. Increasingly, social media networks are making you *pay* to reach your audience.

When you take all of these elements together, you have an author platform that you can use to promote your books and communicate with readers. Your platform grows in value over time, so the sooner you build it, the better.

How do I build an author website?

Websites scare newbie writers, but they shouldn't. As I write this, it has never been easier in the history of the internet to create a website. You can have a functional website up and running in less than an hour... yet I still talk to writers who think that they need to learn how to program so they can build their website from scratch.

If you're a web developer by trade, then program to your heart's content. But if you're not a web developer by trade (which I assume you're not because you're still reading this), then don't program your own website. Here's why:

- Web development is a profession. People go to school for it and spend many hours learning it. Your time is better spent writing.
- The tech industry moves at light-speed. You don't have the bandwidth to keep up with browser updates, security vulnerabilities, operating system updates, and more.
- Anything you create is likely to look inferior to what you can already get for free on the internet. Your goal is to be professional. I haven't met a writer yet who has developed a

professional-looking website by themselves. Usually, the website looks like it was created in 1999.

Creating a good website is easy. All you need is the right information. Here are the steps:

Step #1: Decide if you want a WordPress website, a WordPress alternative, or a custom-built website. WordPress is the most common website content management system in the world. It was created originally for blogs, but no, you don't need a blog to have a WordPress site. There is a free version (Wordpress.com) and a paid version, which requires you to buy hosting (Wordpress.org). I highly recommend Wordpress.org. It's inexpensive and it gives you more flexibility. Wordpress.com is free, but you don't own your content, and I always recommend that you own your content. With Wordpress.org, you own your content and can export it and move it at any time.

If you choose Wordpress.org, you need a theme, which is the overall look and feel of your site. Some themes have special features too. You can buy a theme cheaply at a website like Elegant Themes, Theme Forest, or the Envato Market, usually for less than $100. Once you buy a theme, you can install it in just a couple of minutes.

That said, WordPress is not for everyone. There are alternatives, such as Wix, Weebly, and Squarespace that provide compelling alternatives to the WordPress format. Your choice.

If you don't like any of those options, you can find a website developer on ALLi's Service Ratings Directory or a site like Upwork to create your own custom website. This is significantly more expensive, but it gives you the most flexibility. Personally, I wouldn't recommend this until you've had a website for a few years so that you can figure out what works best for you and your readers.

Step #2: Decide on a hosting provider to house your website. There are many hosting providers out there, such as GoDaddy, Bluehost, Host Gator, Dreamhost, etc. There are always new companies entering the space, so I recommend doing a simple internet search. Most providers will charge you for your domain name plus annual hosting costs, which is usually between $200 and $300 per year. Some providers will let you have as many websites as you want with no extra costs other than the additional domain names.

The biggest considerations when choosing a hosting provider are "uptime" (what percentage of the time are the servers live; you don't want a provider that is down a lot), whether you can buy a domain through them, whether they offer domain-based email addresses, ease of installing WordPress, the caliber of their customer service, and of course, price.

Step #3: Decide on your domain name. Your domain name is your choice, but it should be easy to remember, easy to say, and easy to spell. After all, you're going to be writing and saying it a lot. Make sure that readers can understand it, even if they don't see it, like when you're giving your website address on a podcast, for example. Domains usually cost around $10–15 per year, or around £8-12.

The next question I usually hear about domains is whether you should select the privacy option. If you go to Whois.net, you can see the owner of any domain name, their real name, and their physical address. That's problematic for a number of reasons: sometimes companies will sell your information or use it to spam you. Worse, you could have a stalker with bad intentions who wants to find you and do harm to you. This is why I recommend buying the extra privacy option for your domain. When you do, your public information will be hidden. It's usually an extra $10–15 per year.

A final word on domains: if you decide on a domain name, buy it immediately if it's available. Someone can and *will* take it if you don't reserve it.

So let's put everything together and recap the exact steps to create your website:

- Decide if you want a WordPress website, a WordPress alternative, or a custom-built website.
- Decide on a hosting provider to house your website.
- Decide on your domain name.

That's it! If you choose a self-hosted WordPress website like I recommend, you can expect to pay about $200–300 per year for hosting ($15–25 per month), $10–$15 per year per domain, maybe a little more for privacy protection, and around $100 for a WordPress theme. This puts your total investment at around $400, which is a great deal.

What pages should I have on my website?

Every author website is different, but at a minimum I recommend:

- A homepage that showcases your newest work and where to find it.
- An about page that tells readers who you are and why they should care.
- A mailing list signup.
- A dedicated page for your books.
- A contact page.
- A shop page where you can sell your books directly to readers.

I recommend keeping your website simple by having just a few pages, especially at first. I also recommend looking at other websites to see what other authors are doing. You might find a few ideas that you can implement on your website.

Should I blog, podcast, or do video?

While I don't know the right answer for you, I don't recommend doing all of them. My advice is to pick one and learn how to get really good at it.

There are so many resources about blogging, podcasting, and video, and you can find them with a simple internet search.

But if you need some help on which medium might be best for you, follow these rules of thumb:

- *Blogging* is generally best for writers who prefer convention and love the art of words. After all, blogging is writing, and you're already writing books, so if you don't want to think too hard about creating content, and writing feels the most natural to you, blogging may be the best choice. The cons of blogging are that people may not want to read more "stuff" from you if they already read your books, since readers already spend a lot of time reading.
- *Podcasting* is generally best for extroverts. If you like to express your ideas, talk to other people, or speak what's on your mind, audio is the perfect medium to do it. The nice part is that people can listen to you while they're multitasking, and it's an intimate medium where it is perhaps the easiest to build trust and connection. It also funnels nicely into audiobook sales. The downside to podcasting is that you have to buy audio equipment and learn the basics of audio editing.
- *Video* is generally best for introverts. I know this sounds counterintuitive, but introverts tend to do well at video because they can create content on their own terms and engage with viewers on their own terms too. That said, it takes a fair amount of confidence to put yourself on camera, and video has a big learning curve because you have to learn how to keep people's attention.

What should I blog, podcast, or make video about?

There's no right or wrong answer, but this is definitely easier if you write nonfiction that has an educational focus. I find that nonfiction writers usually don't have a problem coming up with content: their focus is on helping people learn something.

Fiction writers have the biggest problem with this question. What should a fiction writer talk about? You can only talk about your book so much.

For fiction, I recommend sharing your journey. What's on your mind every week? It doesn't have to be writing related. Maybe it's vacation photos, or talking about other interests you have that dovetail with your writing. The key is to avoid looking scatterbrained.

I have a weekly podcast called "The Writer's Journey." It's a weekly podcast where I talk about what's on my mind, and what it's like to be a part-time writer. It's primarily a podcast for my readers to get to know me on a deeper level. It's like an audio journal of me documenting my journey as a writer. I also promote my books on the show regularly, so it serves as a discovery point for my audience who may not be familiar with my older works.

That's one way of doing it, but there are many other ways. Your only limit is your imagination.

A final note on this: don't start a blog, podcast, or video channel unless you can produce content consistently. Otherwise, you'll just let your audience down. It's better not to make content if you can't maintain a cadence.

Which social media site should I use?

I recommend that you use the social media networks that you enjoy. If you don't like Facebook, then don't use Facebook. Don't listen to people who tell you that you should be everywhere. Nobody has time to be everywhere. It's far better to pick one or two networks and then spend your time and effort there.

If you're new to social media, experiment to see which platforms you like the most and where you are getting the most engagement. Those are the networks to focus on.

What should I post on social media?

Unlike a blog, podcast, or YouTube channel, social media is transient. You can post whatever you want, and the world will forget about it in a couple of days (or minutes!). I believe this is freeing because it means you can have fun and just be yourself.

Post pictures, random thoughts, videos that moved you, drawings, or even rants. Share other people's content. Ask influencers thoughtful questions. Don't be a jerk.

There's no wrong answer to what you should post, and I strongly believe that picking the right social media network is half the battle. It's a lot harder to come up with post ideas if you don't like or know how to use the social media networks you're posting on.

On most networks, content you post on social media will remain on your profile until you delete it, so focus on being thoughtful so that readers who discover you in the future will have interesting content to see when they follow you.

You don't have to post to social media every day. On some networks, consistent posting will help you build a tribe faster, but that's not necessary. Post when you feel like it, and post when you have something valuable to say. That way, people will listen.

Where do I find readers?

I've always believed that the best place to find readers is around other books in your genre or subgenre.

You find them by searching for and reading blog reviews or video reviews of your comparable books, and by advertising on Amazon or Facebook by targeting the readers of your comparables.

You can also find readers by using the right keywords and categories for your book on all the retailers where you publish.

And finally, you can find readers by positioning your product correctly—meaning you have a cover and book description that speaks directly to them. It also helps if you can create solid talking points for your book to use whenever you do media interviews or guest appearances.

Depending on your genre, there may be other avenues available to you to find readers.

I recommend you start with influencers, who are the people leaving reviews and talking about the book publicly. They tend to be book bloggers and social media personalities. If they are willing to take a chance on your book and read it, then you can get it in front of a bigger audience. But influencers receive many, many pitches, so be prepared for rejection. And remember, not everyone will like your book.

Readers also hang out in message boards and communities like Goodreads, but I recommend that writers stay out of those communities. Readers go there to talk about books, not to receive promotions. You don't want to be "that" author who self-promos their book in a community of avid readers, trust me. That will turn readers off.

What's the best way to interact with my fans?

Interact with fans on the terms that work best for you. Some writers like to use social media, live videos, or email newsletters. Others are even more creative.

Choose the method that doesn't burn you out, and invite readers to communicate with you that way.

As a writer (especially if you're an introvert), you owe it to yourself to interact in a way that doesn't burn you out. If Facebook groups give you anxiety, then don't visit them.

Whatever you do, I believe that talking to your fans is a must. Thank each and every reader who promotes your book, answer people's questions, and be genuine. Readers like that.

How should I write my book description?

As a publisher, you need to learn copywriting and how to write sales copy. Writing book descriptions is a specialized technique. If you find yourself summarizing your book's plot, you're doing it wrong.

Look at the bestselling books on Amazon. What are their descriptions like? Become a student of descriptions, pick and choose from the best ones, and incorporate those techniques into your style.

If you are unable to master this skill, you can also hire someone to do it for you, but it will cost a premium.

What is metadata and why is it important for marketing?

Metadata is the information about your book that helps retailers find and classify it.

Your book's title, subtitle, keywords, categories, and book description are metadata, to name a few.

On Amazon, metadata is especially important because it's how the search engine algorithm determines when to display your book. For nonfiction, having relevant words in your title, subtitle, keywords, and book description will help your book get discovered. For fiction, titles aren't as important but the other metadata items can still aid in your book's discovery.

Can I use marketing links in my Kindle book?

Generally speaking, you can use links in your e-book as long as you don't violate the retailer's terms of service. On Amazon, you cannot use Amazon affiliate links to promote your next book. Using Amazon affiliate links of any kind is a violation of the Amazon Associates terms of service.

Other retailers don't like to see links to competitors in e-books. For example, Apple doesn't tolerate Amazon links in e-books they sell. To be safe, always link to your own website if you're going to promote the next book in your series.

. . .

Can I use Amazon affiliate links in my newsletters and autoresponders?

No. Using affiliate links in your emails is a direct violation of the Amazon Associates agreement. Link to your website instead.

My book isn't selling. Why?

It could be a number of things.

- Your cover might be unprofessional or it might not speak to your target audience.
- Your book description could be ineffective and not salesy enough.
- Your book could have typos or poor formatting. Or the story might not resonate with readers because you need to improve your craft.
- You might not be reaching the right readers.
- You might not be advertising or promoting enough.
- It might be that readers just don't want this kind of book. Harsh truth, but it's possible.

You'll never truly know.

Get some opinions from other writers in your genre if you can. Fix what you can afford to fix, if you choose to do so.

Be careful about completely rebranding your cover or rewriting your book too early on. They might not actually be the root cause of your book not selling, and it's an expensive mistake if you make a wrong guess.

If your book isn't selling, you may be better off writing your next book, especially if the next book is in the same series.

Whatever happens, don't get discouraged. Learn from the experience, salvage the situation as best you can, and move forward.

A lot of people have already written books in my genre. Should I write something else?

Write what you're passionate about and what will make you money.

If a genre is crowded, don't let that scare you. It just means that there's a big demand for it. You'll have to study other books in the genre to understand what readers want so you can position your book accordingly. Maybe there's a unique angle you have that the competition doesn't.

I can't find any books similar to mine.

When I was a newbie, I once asked this question to a self-publishing expert. They gave me an ass-kicking answer, and it's the same answer I'm going to give you: you probably haven't found any book like yours because you haven't looked hard enough.

Every book has comparables, even if it's only one or two.

If you have only searched for your book on Amazon or Goodreads, then expand your search. Categories and keywords on Amazon are limited, and authors often have to misclassify their books in order to be discovered. This makes it sometimes difficult to do meaningful market research on Amazon, particularly with fiction.

Search places like Reddit for reader discussions. There are also tools like Tag Mash by Library Thing that allow you to do more specific searches. You will eventually find a book similar to yours. In some respects, finding just one book will tell you a lot. If you have to expend a lot of energy just to find that book, it means there is probably not a demand.

If there are *truly* no other books like yours on the market, it definitely means there isn't a demand. It could mean you're ahead of your time, or it could mean that readers just aren't searching for your kind of book. That doesn't mean you *shouldn't* continue. It just means you should publish with realistic expectations.

How do I get readers to share about my book?

Ask them. Readers want to help you, but they sometimes don't know how.

If you have a mailing list, ask if your readers wouldn't mind sharing your book with a friend who would appreciate it.

Ask them to share your book in the back matter.

Consider a giveaway of some kind to encourage readers to share your book (but be ethical, please).

Thank readers who share your work.

No matter what you do, don't ask too much. You don't want to look desperate and you don't want to shame your readers into helping you. Just let them know you need their help and let them do what they choose to do.

How can I sell books directly on my website?

You can use a site like Gumroad or Payhip to sell books directly to readers from your website. They take a percentage of the sale in exchange for processing the customer's payment card. You keep the rest.

Direct sales for e-books and audiobooks are awesome, especially when your promotional strategy is to lead people to your own website for orders and sales. The commissions are higher, sometimes as high as 90 percent or more, because you're cutting out the intermediary (such as book retailers).

You can use a service like BookFunnel to deliver e-books to your customers with minimal hassle.

For print book direct sales, in the US IngramSpark will ship orders received on your website directly from their warehouses to your reader, as if they came straight from you, saving you the 30% or more commissions taken from a print sale by the online retailers. In countries where this service isn't yet available, you'll have to handle the shipping, so I only recommend direct sales for print if you ship books to customers promptly and make sure you charge enough to adequately ship anywhere in the world, and you offer something special that readers can't get anywhere else, like a signed copy. Otherwise, direct sales for print books may not be worth the time or energy.

At a minimum, I highly recommend implementing direct sales for your e-books. It costs almost nothing to implement.

What should I offer as a freebie to attract a mailing list?

Offer something of value that your readers can't get anywhere else.

For fiction, that could be a short story, novella, or even a full-length novel.

For nonfiction, it could be a checklist, a cheat sheet, or an educational or inspirational audio or video.

The key is to give them something valuable and worth their time.

To do this, you have to create an autoresponder sequence, which brings us to the next question.

Do I need autoresponders for my email list, and how long should they last?

An autoresponder is an email that fires after a subscriber joins your mailing list, according to certain conditions. The most common reason for an autoresponder is to deliver a free gift. You can set an autoresponder to fire immediately when someone signs up for your list, and you can put links in the email of where subscribers can download their gift. That's a classic use of an autoresponder.

Autoresponders have other uses as well. For example, you might want a sequence of welcome emails to go to your new subscribers once they join your list, at an interval of once a week for three weeks. Or maybe you want to send them a certain email if they click a link in one of your newsletters.

In any case, an autoresponder sequence introduces readers to you and your work. They're a great way to engage readers and bring them up to speed with what you're currently doing.

Autoresponders are called different terms, depending on your email list provider. Aweber calls them follow-ups, for example. But the concept is the same. An autoresponder differs from a newsletter because they are automated. You have to actively send a newsletter to your subscribers. An autoresponder works without you having to do anything apart from the initial setup.

My personal opinion is that autoresponders are essential. Think of them like little employees working on your behalf.

The next question is what type of autoresponder sequence works best for you. At a minimum, I think a welcome sequence of 2-3 weeks is a good idea.

In the first email, deliver your freebie. Set it so that it delivers immediately upon signup.

In the second email, follow up and ask readers if they received their free gift. Sometimes your first email may get tangled up in spam filters. Set this email to fire a few days after signup.

In the third email, formally introduce yourself and tell readers what to expect on the list. Have fun with this email and let your personality shine! Promote one of your books at the end. Set this to fire approximately one week after signup.

If you decide to keep going, have fun. Once a week is probably the most I'd send an autoresponder. After a few weeks, people get tired of emails, so I wouldn't make your sequence too long.

Help! My email list subscribers are unsubscribing.

It's natural to have a few unsubscribers as you go along, but if you're losing a lot of subscribers, or your emails aren't being opened, something is wrong. People unsubscribe from lists because the emails don't provide the value they want. A high unsubscribe rate indicates your emails aren't promising what you delivered, or that they are boring.

Brush up on your copywriting skills. Rewrite your autoresponders with a clear call to action at the end.

Sometimes your email service provider will ask subscribers why they wish to unsubscribe. Figure out why they're leaving.

The good news is that this is usually an easy problem to fix.

My email list subscribers aren't opening my emails.

Your subject lines need work. Work on getting readers' attention. A boring subject line like "New book release" could be something like "Ka POW! I just launched a new book!"

Some email providers will also let you split test subject lines if your list is big enough. Do that if you can and test several subject lines, because sometimes you never know what will convert better.

Another reason your subscribers may not be opening your emails is because you haven't emailed them in a long time, so they may have moved on.

If you send repeated regular emails and your open rates are still bad (less than 50 percent), consider removing people from your list who haven't opened your emails in the last six months. Every email list provider has tools to help you do this.

BOOK PROMOTION

How do I promote my first book?

Typically for a first-time author, gaining the right readers for your book is the primary goal. As an unknown author, getting your book into the hands of new readers, who can then share it with their friends, talk about it on social media, and go on to buy your other books, is the most important outcome of a promotion.

If you're writing a fiction series, you'll want to hold back on your promotion until you have at least two books published. Many readers don't like to invest in a series until they know it will continue. Sometimes writers quit series or die before finishing them, so readers don't like to get burned. Having at least a couple of books shows that you're serious.

Also, paid advertising may not work as well with only one book, since there isn't anything for readers to buy when they finish your story.

If you have a series and are publishing the first book, I'd say definitely let your mailing list and social media channels know about the book, and I would seek as many reviews as you can get. But I might hold off on Facebook or Amazon ads until the second book to ensure you get the most value out of your ads. That's a personal preference.

If you write fiction standalones or nonfiction, then it makes sense to put your full force into marketing and promotion right away since you have a "complete" product.

There is a school of thought that using Amazon KDP Select for your first book is a good idea to gain access to Amazon's marketing tools. Amazon is the largest book and e-book retailer. Ensuring that your book sells well on Amazon is key to overall success.

On the other hand, if your long-term strategy is to build a business on your own website, then you are best to start slowly and build over time, creating your own real estate and email list.

See the low-cost book promotion strategies at the end of this chapter.

How do I get well-known authors to endorse my book?

It helps if you know them, but if you don't, you'll have to email them to pitch them on the idea.

Keep your email brief and to the point, and make the ask very clear.

I also recommend only asking authors in your genre.

Some authors don't do endorsements, so be prepared for rejection. After all, they don't know you and they may not have time to read your book. Offer to send them the first chapter so they can see the quality of your work.

If you're a new author, you might not get any endorsements. But if you keep building a portfolio, you'll get an endorsement at some point.

Should I hire a publicist?

PR services are expensive, and it's not likely that they'll generate a return on your investment. For this reason, I would be wary of any service that says it can guarantee a return on your money, as it may be an unscrupulous provider.

Should you decide to use a PR firm, check to see if it's listed in the ALLi Service Ratings Directory first.

How should I price my book to sell more?

Price promotion is the act of putting concentrated marketing activity around a title for a short period of time while the title is free or priced cheaply. There are three main goals that authors have in mind when deciding to run a price promotion:

• Gaining new readers.

• Generating reviews.

• Spiking revenue.

While the three are interrelated, your primary goal will decide how you price your book, so it's important to enter into a promotion with one in mind.

It's important to start somewhere, and make modifications as you go, so don't get hung up on getting it perfect the first time. Just set a price and see.

When you're starting out, it could be that getting your work into the world is more important than how much money it makes. You might set your book at a low price or give it away free to get your work seen and into the hands of the right readers, so your first project sets you up for your second.

Most publishers find that second and third projects sell better or are more profitable. If you have a series, consider pricing the first book lower as a loss leader. It's not uncommon to see Book One at $2.99 and sequels at $3.99 or higher. The idea is that you can make up for the lower commissions on Book One by pricing the sequels slightly higher.

Take some time to do a competitive analysis. Look at similar-length books in your genre and evaluate what the standard price range is. You'll want to fit somewhere within the standard price range while taking into account what makes your book stand out.

How long should a book promotion last?

Work toward focusing all activity into a three to four-day period, as that will give you enough time to effectively promote and adjust—and it plays to Amazon's algorithmic preference toward recency.

Should I give away free books?

There's also permafree pricing, where you can offer Book One for free. At the time of this writing, Amazon doesn't allow free pricing, but if you set your book's price on other retailers to free, then Amazon will price-match the book.

Back in the early days of self-publishing, permafree Book Ones helped some writers sell a *lot* of sequels, and it even helped some writers quit their jobs and make a full-time living from their books.

However, due to algorithm changes, permafree isn't as powerful as it used to be, and I recommend charging money for your work, as you'll attract better readers. Free readers tend to leave harsher reviews, and many tend to only read free and not go on to buy. While some retailers like Apple and Kobo are favorable to free books, Amazon suppresses free books' visibility.

e-books in the range $0.99 to $1.99 are bargain and discount prices. I recommend using these as promotional price points.

Are book contests good ways to promote my book?

There are many literary and author contests that promise money and prestige for winning works.

However, ALLi's experience has been that some of these contests may not be worth it. In fact, ALLi's Watchdog Desk keeps track of author contests and rates them accordingly!

Here are ALLi's guiding principles when evaluating author awards and contests, taken directly from ALLi's Self-Publishing Advice Center:

1. **The event exists to recognize talent, not to enrich the organizers.** Avoid events which are driven by excessive entry fees, marketing services to entrants, or selling merchandise like stickers and certificates.

2. **Receiving an award is a significant achievement.** An event that hands out awards like Halloween candy dilutes the value of those awards, rendering them meaningless. Beware events that offer awards in dozens of categories. These are often schemes to maximize the number of winners in order to sell them stickers and other merchandise.

3. **The judging process is transparent and clear.** Watch out for contests whose judging criteria and personnel are vague or undisclosed.

4. **Prizes are appropriate and commensurate with the entry fees collected.** If a cash prize is offered, it should align with the size of the entry fee. "Exposure" is not an appropriate prize. Representation or publication are acceptable prizes, but only if offered by a reputable company without hidden fees.

5. **Entrants are not required to forfeit key rights to their work.** Avoid contests with onerous terms, especially those which require the forfeiture of publishing rights without a termination clause. When in doubt, have an independent professional review the terms.

How do I deliver advance reading e-book copies to my readers for a promotion?

I recommend Book Funnel to deliver review copies to your readers. Book Funnel will help readers sideload e-books onto their reading devices. They even provide customer service so you don't have to get involved. Book Funnel is affordably priced too.

Otherwise, you'll have to provide links on where readers can download the book, give clear and detailed instructions on how to sideload the book onto their device, and provide customer service to any readers who get stuck. It can be done, but be prepared to spend time and energy on it.

What's the step-by-step process for obtaining book reviews?

Step one: Find book bloggers in your genre, either through a web search or by looking at reviewers who have already reviewed books in your subgenre.

Step two: Find out how that reviewer likes to be contacted (if they even want to be contacted at all).

Step three: Respect the reviewer's guidelines and make your pitch. If they prefer email, explain what your book is about in a sentence or two and why they might be interested in it. Do your research; if they've read and liked books similar to yours, mention those books in your pitch.

That's it. This is a numbers game. If you email 100 book bloggers, you'll be lucky if ten respond, and luckier if five leave a review.

And of course, be sure to ask your mailing list if they would like review copies. Your readers are far more likely to review your books since they already know you.

Oh, and please, never, *ever* pay for customer reviews. Ever! Not only does it violate every retailer's terms of service, it's unethical.

When promoting my book, is it better to send readers to a book page or directly to my book sales page on Amazon, Google, iBooks, etc.?

It's difficult to know what a reader's preference is when you promote your book. You don't know if they're Amazon customers or Kobo customers, or if they read e-book, paper, or audio, or what country they live in.

For this reason, I recommend sending people to a book page on your website that has links to all of the major retailers, including your own website shop, so they can choose the venue and format they most prefer. It's more thoughtful and it will lead to more sales.

A lot of US authors default to sharing Amazon.com links, but in doing that, they're sending readers to the US version of Amazon. Readers outside the US can't buy on Amazon.com.

What's a solid book launch plan?

First, write the best book you possibly can.

Second, make sure the packaging is as good as you can make it (cover, formatting, book description, metadata).

Third, start talking about the book early and often on your author platform, without being too spammy or annoying. Ask other writers if they are willing to help you promote the book.

Fourth, line up as many advance readers as you can, if you have an existing audience. Send your book to them with at least a few weeks' lead time to read and review the book. Use snippets from reviews on your product page to help promote the book.

Fifth, create Amazon and/or Facebook ads.

Sixth, stack a few ads at book promo sites around your launch to build some early momentum (but remember my advice about not paying too much for advertising if this is your first book).

Of course there are many more promo activities you can take on to launch a book but that's a solid a launch plan and each of these steps is a basic you should implement.

· · ·

Should I issue a press release for my book launch?

Probably not. Press releases take time and energy to craft, and writing them is an art. Press releases are for traditional media outlets, and the sad truth is most of these outlets are unfriendly to indies.

I don't think it's an effective use of your time to court traditional media unless you have a book that would clearly do well on those channels, like a unique cookbook, health book, or other nonfiction book that is likely to result in feature coverage.

What are the best low-cost promotion strategies for authors?

Sometimes the best promotion tactics are low cost or free. Here are some ideas that cost little to nothing.

• Ask other writers to collaborate and share your book.

• Ask book bloggers for reviews.

• Assemble a street team to leave early reviews and help you spread the word about the book.

• Create an autoresponder sequence that promotes your books to new mailing list subscribers.

• Enroll temporarily in KDP Select and take advantage of some increased visibility with its promotional tools (but don't stay forever!).

• Use promotional tools at retailers like Kobo and distributors like PublishDrive. They offer free opportunities to promote your book. Sometimes they charge a modest fee.

• Use a book promo site to promote your book to a mailing list of dedicated readers. These sites often charge affordable fees.

• For fiction writers: write short stories in your book's world and send them to literary magazines to see if they will publish them. Use a site like Ralan.com to find magazines that will pay you for your work.

• Use Amazon Ads. They're cheap and effective.

Those are just a few ideas. With some creativity, you can find many others!

PART VI

BOOK RIGHTS AND LICENSING

COPYRIGHT AND CONTRACTS

Why is copyright important?

Copyright is one of the main types of intellectual property. It allows the copyright owner to protect against others copying or reproducing their work. Copyright affords an author the exclusive legal right to publish, perform, or record a literary work, to profit from it, and to authorize others to do the same.

Copyright law, policy, and practice underwrite the publication and sale of books. The income that every author and publisher receives derives from copyright law.

There is no international copyright law. It varies by country and is enforced more in some countries than others. In the United States and Europe, copyright law entitles the author to commissions and royalties for their lifetime plus 70 years.

That copyright has real and significant value can be seen in how it is ever more vehemently contested by three competing interests:

- **Big Tech:** Internet-based publishing platforms like Google,

Facebook and Amazon that authors use to publish and/or promote books.

- **Big Content:** Global media corporations like Penguin Random House, News International, and Hollywood to which authors license publishing rights. Here we also find large self-publishing services like Author Solutions (the subject of an ALLi Watchdog Advisory, applied when an organization fails to meet ALLi's standards for ethics and excellence). Some of these companies grab rights as well as charge service fees.
- **Big Legal:** Large legislating territories and blocs like the United States or the European Union who aim to modify the power of Big Tech and Big Content.

Independent authors who are both writers and publishers, and who actively manage their own publishing rights, need to understand the importance of copyright and how to assert their rights in the digital age.

ALLi answers the most important copyright questions in our *Copyright Bill of Rights* campaign book, which also asserts eight fundamental rights for authors.

What are the eight rights in ALLi's Copyright Bill of Rights?

1. The Right to Operate

2. The Right to Link, License, and Collaborate

3. The Right to Fair Remuneration

4. The Right to Equitable Fair Dealing/Fair Use Frameworks

5. The Right to Defend Copyright

6. The Right to Coherence and Transparency

7. The Right to Recognition in Machine-Generated Books

8. The Right to Copyright Education

You will find the Bill of Rights in ALLi's member zone, where it's free to our members, or you can purchase it at selfpublishingadvice.org/bookshop.

Should I copyright my work?

The short answer is that your work is copyrighted the moment you affix it to the page. You don't have to take any additional action to copyright your work.

Some countries such as the United States *do* ask that authors register their copyrights with the government, however. If your country offers this option, I recommend it, even though there is usually a small fee associated with it. In the United States, registering your work protects you if you need to file a lawsuit for copyright infringement, and it gives you access to more monetary damages.

My book idea is taken. Should I quit writing my work in progress?

It can be disheartening to see that your book idea has already been done. I've been in the eleventh hour before publication, only to find out that someone already executed my idea!

As gut-wrenching as it may feel, it's OK. Copyright is in the expression of the work for a reason. That's what's most important to readers.

Readers won't care that somebody else has written about your topic. In fact, it's quite the opposite. Think about the readers who love the other book. They probably want to read more books like it, which means you are a hero because your book meets their needs.

Once your book is out, you might even reach out to the other author and see if you can collaborate on a promotion. This can be a win-win situation.

Can I use a song lyric, quote, or another person's work in my book?

No, unless you have the content creator's permission.

Songs are copyrighted, and it is expensive to get permission from a record label to use famous song lyrics.

Quotes are also copyrighted.

The general rule of thumb is to always ask permission before using another's content in your work. If you can't get permission, don't use the content.

When do I need to attribute the creator of a copyrighted work?

Let's say you want to use an image on your blog.

First off, get permission from the image creator. You cannot simply download the image and start using it—it's copyrighted.

Many works have a Creative Commons license that governs how you can use the work, which is helpful. You can use a site like Creative Commons Search to find images to use. Be sure to follow the Creative Commons license, though—if the license requires attribution to the creator, be sure to give attribution. When in doubt, always give the creator a shout out!

If you prefer to avoid Creative Commons, you can purchase royalty-free images (also known as stock images) from sites like Shutterstock. Many of these sites offer plans where you can buy a la carte or download a certain number of images per month.

There are also websites for royalty-free stock videos, audio, and other types of content.

If I make a change to my book, do I need to copyright it again?

Generally speaking, if you live in a country where you have to register your copyright, you don't need to register a new copyright if you make minor changes to your book, such as to correct typos.

If you make enough changes to warrant a new edition of the book (as I discussed in the Production chapter), then it is best to also register a new copyright since much of the content will be different and will therefore benefit from a new registration.

Can I use trademarked company names or products in my book?

A trademark identifies and distinguishes a company or product in the marketplace. A classic example is the Coca-Cola logo and its slogan "Share a Coke." If you see those on a can of soda, you know you're looking at a Coca-Cola product. If you manufacture soda, and you create a similar logo or slogan that makes customers think you are Coca-Cola, that's trademark infringement because Coca-Cola will likely be harmed by losing customers.

Generally speaking, companies like to protect their names and products. They typically like to approve any mention of their brands, even in books. This is because they want to control their brands and anything associated with them.

Avoid using any trademark in your book's title or subtitle. That is direct trademark infringement because it could confuse customers into thinking that your book is affiliated with the trademark. For example, if you write interactive novels, you can't call them *Choose Your Own Adventures* because that term is trademarked.

I would also avoid using trademarked company names or products in your book's keywords to avoid any allegations of trademark infringement.

Using trademarks in your book's manuscript is a different story.

Sometimes, using brand names in the text of your manuscript is unavoidable. This is particularly true with nonfiction. For example, it would be almost impossible to write a book about car repairs without mentioning car brands. You can't write a corporate history of Google without referencing its products. That kind of reference is OK.

In fiction, I would avoid using trademarks in your book's text whenever possible. Instead of Coke, say cola. Instead of Levi's, say jeans. It makes for better writing. Using brand names detracts from the story.

Trademarks can also date your work. Companies go out of business, product lines go out of style, and the names you mention in your book today might be unrecognizable to future readers, which makes for a poorer reading experience.

Which publishing contract clauses ring alarm bells?

Let's say you've just received an offer to publish your book, perhaps from one of the big traditional publishers (Penguin Random House or Hachette, for example).

Which clauses should you look out for?

The good news is that ALLi has a fair number of resources to help you look out for the most deadly clauses. Check the Resources section for more information.

I'll cover my personal top three.

A do not compete clause bars an author from publishing any additional work that might compete with the book that the publisher is creating.

The purpose of a do not compete clause is to protect the publisher's work. For example, if an author self-published a book in the same genre around the same time as the publisher's, then readers might buy the self-published book and not the traditionally published one, thus hurting the publisher's sales.

Do not compete clauses can be quite draconian. Indie authors need to check the implications of such a clause on their self-published work and negotiate accordingly. It's usually possible to publish under a different pen name, usually in a different genre. Otherwise, the publisher could legally enforce the clause.

It goes without saying that a do not compete clause can severely cripple a writer's business by restricting what they can publish. Strike it out of the contract, and argue that it is inappropriate for an indie author. If the publisher won't budge, I would walk away.

A termination or reversion of rights clause states what happens if one party fails to uphold their obligations, and what happens to the author's copyright as a result.

If a publisher goes bankrupt, what happens to the author's copyright? What if a conglomerate acquires the publisher? What if a book just isn't selling and the author wants the rights back so they can self-publish? What if the publisher fails to publish the book in the first place, or if the author decides not to provide the manuscript, or doesn't agree with the editing, or virtually any other scenario that could go wrong?

The termination and reversion of rights clause addresses that. As a general rule, every termination and reversion clause is different. One of your many goals in a rights negotiation should be to get rights reversion as quickly as possible. In the early days of self-publishing, there were many stories of traditionally published writers whose books weren't selling. The authors wanted the rights back but couldn't get them because of contracts they signed decades ago. Don't let that happen to you.

The grant of rights clause outlines what rights the author is signing over to the publisher. You want to avoid granting all your rights. Instead, limit the grant of rights as much as possible to strictly those rights the publisher needs and plans to use. Sometimes grant of rights clauses can be overly broad and will take rights that you didn't think of without enumerating those rights or compensating you for them.

YOUR BOOK, YOUR RIGHTS

What are publishing rights?

The right to produce or reproduce a book in any format—as a reprint, or a movie, or in translation—is a publishing right. Publishing rights are typically granted by an author to a rights buyer such as a TV or film producer (or publisher) in the form of a license that grants permission for a specific use.

As ALLi's legal advisor Helen Sedwick puts it, imagine that your book is a shopping center, and you are the landlord. Each empty shop represents a set of rights. One shop might be print books in English, another might be audiobooks in Spanish, another might be e-books in Mandarin, another might be movie rights, another TV rights, another audio drama, and so on. If your book becomes mega successful, your shopping center might even, like Harry Potter, include a theme park.

Since your rent depends entirely on how much each shop sells, you want to rent to companies that have the wherewithal to use those particular rights to make money for you both. In other words, you shouldn't grant rights to the French translation of your book to an English-only publisher that is unlikely to exploit them.

"Exploit" is the term you want to understand. Smart authors and publishers *exploit* opportunities to license their copyrights.

As you learn about, and begin to exploit, your publishing rights, keep the landlord analogy in mind. "Use it or lose it" is the proper attitude for authors to have toward rights buyers (including publishers). In any negotiation, you as the author will want to limit the term, territory, and formats that you are offering to the buyer.

How do authors sell their books for film, television, etc.?

In order to sell your book—or more correctly license your rights—to film or TV producers, it's important to understand how rights are traded and licensed, and how to negotiate a good deal. Fortunately, ALLi has written a book on this topic! It's called *How Authors License Publishing Rights: ALLi's Guide to Working with Publishers, Producers and Others*.

I highly recommend that you check it out if you are interested in licensing your publishing rights, as it goes in depth into the topic.

Essentially you need to pitch your book to rights buyers. This involves a number of skills, from preparing pitch documents to negotiating the deal. Some indies have managed to do this successfully. Others have decided it's not worth the effort. Check out *How Authors License Publishing Rights* to decide what the best path is for you.

How can I find a translator for my book?

Start with the ALLi Service Ratings Directory, which has some vetted, approved, and experienced translators. Another good source is Reedsy.

Quality translation isn't cheap. You'll want a translator who is going to be a partner in bringing your book to a foreign market. You'll also want them to have marketing knowledge for that language, as it's difficult to market a book in a language you don't speak!

I only recommend venturing into translation if your book is selling well enough to afford a translator, which will cost several thousands of dollars, if not more. I would also only recommend a language that has avid readers in your genre. And even then, there are other, better investments you can make before translation, like audio.

Advances in technology are making AI translation ever better. A human translator is still needed to polish the machine translation, but this emerging technology can reduce the overall costs greatly.

Is it advisable to use an agent for foreign rights sales?

You don't need an agent to negotiate foreign rights. In fact, you might be better served doing it yourself.

To learn the basics of contracts and copyright, read ALLi's Guidebook, *How Authors License Publishing Rights: ALLi's Guide to Working with Publishers, Producers and Others.*

You can hire an attorney to look over the contract before you sign it.

You will need to learn to become a wizard negotiator.

An agent can add value and, while reputable agents provide a valuable service, any time you introduce more people into your book publishing process, you make less money.

There's also the opportunity for embezzlement or contractual issues, especially if bad actors are involved.

ALLi has worked with a variety of agencies and other services to negotiate rights sales. Check www.selfpublishingadvice.org frequently to stay up to date on ALLi's efforts in this area.

THE END

RESOURCES TO HELP YOU KEEP LEARNING

We have gathered over seventy helpful resources to help you continue the learning in your author journey.

Please visit www.selfpublishingadvice.org/faqresources to see the list, along with links to the many books, blog articles, and podcast episodes that you'll find helpful.

While you're there, be sure to check out what else our Self-Publishing Advice Center has to offer.

Enjoy, and have fun digging into the content!

ACKNOWLEDGEMENTS

Special thanks to the ALLi Leadership Team for their help and support in the creation of this book. An especially hearty thank you to our incredible members who have asked many of the questions answered in this book.

Editorial: Margaret Hunter at Daisy Editorial

Cover Design: JD Smith at JD Smith Design

Index: Amron Gravett of Wild Clover Book Services.

ABOUT ALLI

THE ALLIANCE OF INDEPENDENT AUTHORS

This book is one of a number of self-publishing guidebooks for authors produced by the Alliance of Independent Authors (ALLi). ALLi is pronounced "ally" and the organisation is an ally to self-publishers across the globe, where all (ALL) work for one (i) and one for all.

ALLi is a non-profit professional and business association for indie authors. Its mission is to foster ethics and excellence in self-publishing, by helping its members to become great publishers and by helping to advance the place of indie authors in the publishing and literary sectors. All profits are reinvested back into the organization for the benefit of its members and the wider author community.

As an ALLi member, you're not just joining a membership and advocacy organization, you're joining a movement. Whether you're self-publishing your first novel or your fiftieth, ALLi is with you every step of the way, with a suite of member benefits that includes free guidebooks, discounts and deals, member forums, contract consultancy, advisory board, literary agency, watchdog and more.

The biggest benefit of all is access to ALLi's supportive, dynamic community of team, advisors and successful indie authors and authoritative advice you can trust.

If you haven't yet, is it time you joined?

Allianceindependentauthors.org

**Alliance of
Independent
Authors**

MORE BOOKS IN THIS SERIES

For a comprehensive overview of self-publishing, check out the rest of ALLi's Publishing Guides for Authors series. They cover all you need to know from the moment you finish your final draft manuscript to the moment when you have established yourself as a working authorpreneur, earning your living from writing books as an indie author.

Learn more about ALLi's guidebooks by visiting www. selfpublishingadvice.org/guidebooks.

MEET THE AUTHOR: M.L. RONN

Science fiction and fantasy on the wild side!
M.L. Ronn (Michael La Ronn) is the author of many science fiction and fantasy novels. He also hosts a weekly YouTube channel for writers, Author Level Up. In 2012, a life-threatening illness made him realize that storytelling was his number one passion. He's devoted his life to writing ever since, making up whatever story makes him fall out of his chair laughing the hardest. Every day.

Resources for Writers
www.authorlevelup.com , Michael@authorlevelup.com

Fiction
www.michaellaronn.com

MEET THE SERIES EDITOR: ORNA ROSS

Orna Ross is an award-winning and bestselling novelist and poet and founder-director of the Alliance of Independent Authors (ALLi), the global nonprofit association for self-publishing authors. This advocacy work for indie authors has seen her named "one of the 100 most influential people in publishing" by UK publishing trade magazine *The Bookseller* alongside many other honors.

Orna publishes widely across fiction, nonfiction, and poetry while running ALLi and her publishing business from the Free Word Centre in London, "a home for organizations interested in who gets to speak and be heard in society."

MORE ADVICE

We'd love to send you a weekly roundup
of self-publishing advice
from our award-winning blog.

Sign up here for the best tips and tools from the Alliance of Independent Authors

Delivered to your inbox each Wednesday

WE'D LOVE YOUR FEEDBACK
REVIEW REQUEST

If you enjoyed this book, would you consider leaving a brief review online on your favorite online bookstore that takes reviews: Amazon, Apple, Barnes and Noble or <u>Goodreads</u>?

A good review is very important to authors these days as it helps other readers know this is a book worth their time.

It doesn't have to be long or detailed. Just a sentence saying what you enjoyed and a star-rating is all that's needed. Many thanks.

150 Self-Publishing Questions Answered:
ALLi's Writing, Publishing, and Book Marketing Tips for Indie Authors and Poets

© M.L. Ronn. 2020

ebook: 978-1-913349-88-2
Paperback: 978-1-913349-89-9
Large Print: 978-1-913349-90-5
HB: 978-1-913349-91-2
Audio: 978-1-913349-92-9

AUTHOR ENQUIRIES: INFO@AUTHORLEVELUP.COM
PUBLISHING ENQUIRIES: INFO@ORNAROSS.COM

"To go creative return to the font."

FONT PUBLICATIONS IS THE PUBLISHING IMPRINT
FOR ORNA ROSS FICTION & POETRY
AND
ALLIANCE OF INDEPENDENT AUTHORS
PUBLISHING GUIDES FOR AUTHORS & POETS

ALL FONT BOOKS—FICTION, NON-FICTION AND POETRY—HAVE THE SAME INTENTION AT
SOURCE:
TO INSPIRE INDEPENDENCE, FREEDOM AND IMAGINATIVE CONNECTION.
ALL ENQUIRIES: INFO@ORNAROSS.COM

Made in the USA
Las Vegas, NV
02 October 2021

31521725R10116